ANCIENT MYTHS
AND
THE NEW ISIS MYSTERY

ANCIENT MYTHS
AND
THE NEW ISIS MYSTERY

Seven lectures given in Dornach
4 to 13 January 1918
and a lecture given in Dornach
24 December 1920

RUDOLF STEINER

& Anthroposophic Press

Translated by M. Cotterell from shorthand notes unrevised by the lecturer. Translation revised by Mado Spiegler. The original German text of the seven lectures on ancient myths was published under the title *Alte Mythen und ihre Bedeutun* (vol. 180 in the Bibliographical Survey, 1961) by the Rudolf Steiner Nachlassverwaltung, Dornach, Switzerland. The lecture on the Isis-Sophia was translated by James H. Hindes. The original German text of this lecture was published under the title *Die Brucke zwischen der Weltgeistgkeit und dem physischen im Menschen* (lecture 14, vol. 202 in the Bibliographical Survey) by the Rudolf Steiner Nachlassverwaltung, Dornach, 1970.

Published in the United States by Anthroposophic Press,
R.R. 4, Box 94 A-1, Hudson, New York 12534.

LIBRARY OF CONGRESS CATALOGING-IN-PUBLICATION DATA

Steiner, Rudolf, 1861–1925.
[Selections. English. 1994]
Ancient myths and the New Isis mystery / Rudolf Steiner.
p. cm.
"Seven lectures given in Dornach, 4th to 13th January, 1918,
and a lecture given on December 24, 1920."
ISBN 0-88010-377-9 (pbk.)
1. Anthroposophy. 2. Mythology. I. Title.
BP595. S894213 1994
299'.935—dc20 93–47531
CIP

10 9 8 7 6 5 4 3 2 1

Printed in the United States of America

CONTENTS

The nature of mythical thinking. Egyptian concern with soul experience after death expressed in Isis-Osiris myth. Egyptian and Greek myths reflect shared consciousness about spiritual matters. Three generations of Greek gods. Human beings not created by gods in Greek myths. Intuition, Inspiration, Imagination. Salt, Mercury, Sulphur.

Development of consciousness reflected in myths. Osiris myth reflects change from picture writing to letter script. Myths express human physiological wisdom. Puberty once experienced as change of consciousness. Forces underlying feeling of nationalism. Development of abstract thought. The sign of the cross.

Moral impulse enters when Old Testament God is seen as creator of human beings. Osiris myth means that human beings once directly experienced spiritual through Imaginations. The veil of Isis. The legend of the New Isis. Need to regain the power of the Word. Eulenspiegelism. Becoming older consciously.

Human evolution and the Mystery of Golgotha. The sun and Christ. The Christian meaning of the Isis-Osiris myth. Lucifer and Ahriman in Egyptian and modern civilizations. Sophia and the Mystery of Golgotha. Sophia has been lost in space. Sophia wisdom needed so that Christ may appear before us. The Christmas festival.

INTRODUCTION

In this series of lectures Rudolf Steiner repeatedly challenges us to awaken a new way of thinking that can truly
penetrate into the social questions surrounding us. As he
so often did, Steiner emphasizes how spiritual science can,
indeed must, address the pressing issues of the day. It
might seem strange to some readers that a book with the
title *Ancient Myths* should be a call to a new understanding
of our modern condition, yet it is through an appreciation
of the significance of myths in the lives of ancient peoples
that Steiner makes clear the challenges we face in our
modern ways of knowing.

The ancient myths are an expression of great truths
about the nature of the universe and human development.
In mysterious, image-filled ways they describe a people's
knowledge of their origins, and also of their particular
state of consciousness. The different myths gave ancient
people pictures of their development—of their gains and
losses in human becoming—and helped them to understand their place within the evolving universe.

These stories challenge us to exercise a consciousness
other than our modern one if we want to experience their
truths. We must, for example, try to imagine what the different circles of the gods meant to a Greek, or how the slaying of Osiris spoke to the experience of an Egyptian. This

entering into another kind of consciousness—where the pictures express living realities and speak of real experiences of a macrocosmic-microcosmic relationship—is particularly difficult for modern people. Steiner articulates how the ideas, the words, and even the pictures in the ancient myths have become abstractions for us, cut off from any sense of the experiences that they actually represent. And so the real thrust of these lectures is to encourage us to develop a thinking which can reunite us again to the realities beyond our narrow, abstracted understandings.

Steiner looks to the myths of neighboring cultures—of the ancient Egyptians, Greeks, and Israelites—to illustrate how myths express the particular mode of consciousness of a people. He makes many fascinating connections and comparisons, exploring the heritage that different mythologies have contributed to our present world conceptions. Students of mythology will find rich insights in these lectures.

The Egyptian Osiris-Isis story is particularly interesting to Steiner in these lectures. He sees Osiris as an expression of the Egyptian experience of the loss of direct Imagination of the supersensible world. With the slaying of Osiris the Egyptians expressed that "the forces active in the old clairvoyance are now amidst the dead . . . imaginative clairvoyance disappeared from earth as a normal faculty of the human soul." This living, direct picture-knowing was replaced by ever greater abstraction: Isis discovered Osiris's corpse in Phoenicia, where writing originated as a transformation of the earlier picture-script.

Steiner draws attention especially to the relationship between the loss of imaginative consciousness as experienced by the Egyptians and the challenge we face today to bring new life to our abstract ways of thinking. Here, as in other lecture cycles (particularly *Egyptian Myths and Mysteries*), he points to the connections between the Egypto-Chaldean historical epoch and our own. Certain impulses that were experienced in ancient Egypt reappear today in a new form.

In the third lecture, Steiner refers to the experience that the Egyptians had of Isis as "the epitome of all the deepest thoughts the Egyptians were able to form about the archetypal forces working in nature and in the human being." He describes a statue of Isis in the ancient temple at Sais, beneath which was the inscription: "I am the All, I am the Past, the Present, and the Future; no mortal has lifted my veil." He describes how for the early Egyptians this use of the word "mortal" meant that only one who had awakened to the immortal spiritual life of the soul could lift the veil of Isis.

Steiner then tells a new story, a new Osiris-Isis legend. This is a truly remarkable story, and one which I believe is of great importance for our time. Steiner tells it with great care, and with, for him, surprising tentativeness. As he says, "it is in no way born out of foolish arrogance, it is born in humility; it is also of such a nature that perhaps it can only be related today in a most imperfect way."

This story takes place in the land of Philisterium, in the age of scientific profundity. We meet the New Isis as an invisible, sleeping figure, veiled behind a statue of the Representative of Humanity and various adversarial beings. And here, too, is an inscription: "I am the Human Being, I am the Past, the Present, and the Future. Every mortal should lift my veil."

This strange and illusive story is filled with powerful images. It pictures many elements that remind us of the realities of our modern age: a kind of homelessness, the single mother dragging her child through life, the unknown father, the broken child, the attraction of illusion, the power of mechanical laws, cloning, computer paper, and the need for a new relationship to nature. But most of all it challenges us to wake up to experiences and ways of knowing that go beyond our everyday abstract consciousness.

Before she can wear a golden crown of genuine substance—the transformation of her ancient cow horns of clairvoyance and profundity—the New Isis must be able to recognize the true nature of her offspring, she must awaken to the true meaning of the Logos as described in St. John's Gospel. Her challenge, and ours, is for "a conscious grasping . . . of what is meant by the Mystery of Golgotha, by the true power of the word."

In a series of lectures given during Christmastime 1920, called "The Search for the New Isis, Divine Sophia," Steiner brings further insights to this New Isis being. In the second lecture—which I am so glad has been printed here as an addition to the present volume—he announces that we must fulfill a New Isis myth for our age. He describes how the ancient Egyptians experienced that even after his death Osiris continued to be with them because Isis had buried him in the earth; this being of the sun would now await them in the world after death. Steiner then suggests that since the Mystery of Golgotha, humanity has not lost the Christ Being; but what we have lost is the ability to know that this sun being is still intimately connected with us and with the destiny of the earth. He says: "It is not the Christ we lack . . . but the knowledge and wisdom of the Christ, the Sophia of the Christ, the Isis of the Christ."

For many years I have pondered the challenges posed by the New Isis myth. Initially I saw it as a fundamental resource for my work on questions of feminine and masculine as qualities interacting in the individual and in society. At this level the myth can be seen as a call to awaken a new relationship to the feminine, so that we may address the imbalances of long years of masculine influence in our ways of thinking and relating to each other and to the earth. (I am not here equating feminine with woman and masculine with man, but rather referring to soul qualities in all human beings.) The New Isis myth is a story that is continuously evolving, and so, too, I believe, is our human capacity to ever more consciously manifest and balance our masculine and feminine sides.

In recent years, feminist scholarship and the archeological discoveries of early matriarchal cultures have fostered a growing interest in ancient forms of Goddess worship. Many people are finding that the Judeo-Christian conceptions of God no longer describe or inspire their personal search for the divine. A movement is developing to rediscover the Goddess as a feminine, some would say less stern and judgmental, face of the Godhead.

It seems to me that the New Isis myth offers something of deep importance to this search. Rather than looking back, and trying somehow to ignore or erase a male conception of God that pervaded human understanding for thousands of years, it looks to a "New" Isis for an understanding of divinity. This evolving spiritual being can only come to her full stature through understanding the Mystery of Golgotha; she must come to know the true nature of her offspring.

What is so exciting about this myth—and all myths, if we can enter into them as expressions of different stages of human consciousness—is that the pictures are dynamic. They inspire human development. The New Isis inscription reads, "I am the Human Being . . ."; here is a new challenge to our human becoming, to how we understand our relationship to the divine world. From this point of view it becomes clear that this new myth is also about much more than a new consciousness of how feminine and masculine qualities interact in us. It is a challenge to human awakening, to each one of us to bear the spirit with ever greater understanding and responsibility.

Rudolf Steiner told the New Isis myth within this lecture cycle given in 1918, but it appears that very few people took any notice of it. Just as the New Isis statue in the myth was veiled behind the group statue, seen by few—and this within a building closed to none but where "far the greater number of people saw nothing at all"—so the myth too seems to have lived veiled within the lectures. Until recently, even among longtime students of Anthroposophy, it was rarely referred to or discussed. It seems particularly timely that the Anthroposophic Press has now republished these lectures.

Beyond the telling of the New Isis myth the lectures have further insights; they are filled with riddles of human existence. Perhaps one can see the myth itself as the central riddle around which Steiner offers clues and builds connections between the starry heavens and our human becoming, between historical development and human psychology. He shows how spiritual science gives the impulse to new questions that can take us beyond the abstractions of our modern knowledge to new experiences of a spirit-filled reality.

Throughout the lectures he looks at examples of pressing social questions of his time, for example, the chaos in Russia in 1918 and the problems of nationalism. Sadly, rising nationalism continues to be of great concern in our present age. Steiner's view of national chauvinism as a manifestation of a kind of psychosexual impulse operative in the wrong sphere is both amusing and enlightening: "Just imagine," he says, if those calling out for national interests "had to realize that what they crave is after all the mating-voice of the cock, however finely decked out in national garments." In instance after instance, he opens up perspectives on problem areas with a challenge to the human will to discover the real possibilities for development in our age, to awaken to our place within the entire cosmos.

In the later lectures of this cycle, Steiner turns to another aspect of the human riddle: the unusual sounding concept of humanity "becoming younger" through the passage of time. Initially Steiner connects this phenomenon to the fact that as humanity has advanced, the natural development of our soul and spirit nature in connection to our physical aging has ceased at an ever earlier age. In ancient times to grow old was also to grow wise. In our present age it is in our twenties that the physical ceases to let us be dependent on it . . . "through our own will power we must make any further advance." In our materialistic age, when a youth culture so dominates popular images of success, Steiner's words ring with significance: "We must learn in a new way how to become old, and we can only do so through spiritual deepening." To awaken rejuvenating forces right through our lives we must continue to experience newness in our consciousness and not feel that learning belongs only to the young. The questions which Anthroposophy can awaken in us foster ongoing learning.

Steiner always returns to the need "to direct our gaze to what is invisible." He explores the twofoldness of the human being in terms of the head with its spherical form as an externally complete image of the whole cosmos, and the body, which develops physically much more slowly, as "only a fragment," as embodying more the supersensible and invisible. He calls us to know our twofold nature and our task within the cosmos: "to know that from the whole universe there flow unconsciously into the head, stimulating its forces, the secrets of the stars, but that all this must be worked upon the whole life through by the rest of the organism, so that a person may conserve it on earth, carry it through death back again into the spiritual world." We must transform head knowledge into heart knowledge, natural science into spiritual science; this is the task of the future.

The importance of this task is not only for human life but for all of earth development. Here Steiner's statements stand in direct contrast to many modern thinkers who consider the human being an insignificant, and largely destructive, part of earth evolution. Steiner actually begs us to develop a new heart life, for only by doing this in our lives on earth can we give back the forces necessary for the future: "In the human race itself rests the future of the earth's existence." He says that we must learn to "feel through" things, merely thinking through them is not enough.

I find this entire lecture cycle an exercise in trying, with Steiner's guidance, to feel my way through the riddle of human existence. He poses a question and then moves around it, offering pictures that quicken imaginations. The lectures themselves serve as a deed, an example of how to enliven concepts that in our modern thinking have been "passed through a sieve" and so live as abstractions. This work of re-enlivening abstractions requires patience; it takes time to feel one's way beyond a surface, materialistic knowledge.

By the end of the lectures it seems even more appropriate that the New Isis myth appears within them. The myth calls us to wake up, to lift the veil to the spirit and know our place within the past, the present, and the future. The lectures elaborate this call and clarify the challenges that face our awakening. But lest we might think that the task of understanding myths is ever complete, Steiner has warned us already on the first page that "myths are accessible from many points of view, and when something has been said about one of them, its content is far from being exhausted."

SIGNE SCHAEFER
January 1994

4 January 1918

IN THE COURSE of my recent public lectures in Switzerland, I have repeatedly said that the knowledge, the way of thinking currently prevailing, and indeed deeply rooted in the human soul, is ill-suited to deal with social and moral life. Present conditions can be restored to a healthy state only if people are able to find their way back to a thinking, a grasp of the universe, that will give what lives in the soul a direct link with reality.

I said that what prevails in the historical, social, and ethical life is, as it were, dreamt, slept-through by humankind, that in any case abstract ideas are ill-suited to firmly grasping the impulses which must be at work in social life. I stated that in earlier times humans had recourse to myths rooted in older, or as we often say, atavistic experiences. They expressed in mythical form their thoughts concerning the world, whatever of the world secrets entered their field of vision. Myths, the contents of mythology, can be viewed in the most manifold ways, and in fact I described earlier a positively magnificent materialistic explanation of myth by Dupuis.

Over the years I have repeatedly examined one or another myth. However, myths are accessible from many points of view, and when something has been said about one of them, its content is far from being exhausted. Again and again, from different standpoints, different things may be asserted in regard to a myth. It would be very useful for our contemporaries to become acquainted with the nature of the mode of thought that underlies mythological representations. For the ideas which people have come to accept about the origin of myths and the creation of mythology belong ultimately to the realm of the modern superficial judgment which is so widespread.

Embedded in the myths are deep truths that are more connected with reality than those truths expressed through the medium of modern natural science about this or that thing. Physiological, biological truths about humanity can be found in the myths, and the origin of what they express rests upon the consciousness of the connection between the human being as microcosm and the macrocosm. In particular, and this will be my subject today and tomorrow, when we look clearly at the nature of the thinking employed in the myths, we can grasp how deeply, or actually how *shallowly*, ordinary modern concepts are concerned with reality. It is useful therefore to recollect sometimes how myths were formed among neighboring peoples of the pre-Christian ages. The ancient Egyptians, the Greeks,and the Israelites were neighbors and very much interconnected culturally. Moreover, one can say that a great part of the thinking that still rules in the soul today is connected with the knowledge of the Egyptians, Greeks, and Israelites as expressed in the form of their myths.

The first myth I would like to discuss but from a very specific standpoint is the Osiris-Isis myth in Egyptian culture. I have already called your attention to Dupuis's contention that the Osiris-Isis myth is nothing more than a clerical lie, that the priests themselves had nothing more in mind than astronomical-astrological events, but had fabricated such a myth for the common people.

It is very interesting to note that the Greeks not only have a number of gods connected with their own life, but have whole generations of gods: the oldest generation being linked with Gaia and Uranus; the next generation with Chronos and Rhea, the Titans and all that is related to them; and the third generation with the successors of the Titans—Zeus and the whole Zeus circle. We shall see that the construction of such god myths springs from a special type of soul.

The Greeks, Israelites, and Egyptians had different conceptions of their connection with the universe. Nevertheless, there was a deep relationship from a number of standpoints, including what I shall take as a basis today. In the age when the Osiris-Isis myth arose as the representative of more profound truths, the Egyptians developed a knowledge which came from a longing to know the deeper foundations of the human soul. They desired in this way to turn their gaze to that element in the human soul which not only lives between birth and death, but which passes through birth and death and remains alive between death and a new birth. Even external perceptions show how the Egyptians— in their preservation of mummies, in their peculiar cult of the dead—turned the eye of the soul to the element in the soul that passes through the gate of death and in a new form experiences new destinies when the human being treads the paths on the other side of death.

What is it in the human being that passes through the gate of death and enters through birth into earthly existence? This question, more or less unconscious and unexpressed, underlay the thought and aspirations of the Egyptians. For it is this eternal, imperishable element (I have said this often in another form) that the Egyptian consciousness associates with the name of Osiris. Now, in order to have a foundation, let us consider the Osiris myth in its most important aspects, as it has been preserved.

It is said that at one time Osiris ruled in Egypt. It is said that the Egyptians owed him principally the suppression of cannibalism, and that they owed him the plough, agriculture, the preparation of food from the plant kingdom, the building of cities, certain legal ideas, astronomy, rhetoric, even writing, and so on. It is said furthermore that Osiris not only introduced these beneficent arts and institutions among the Egyptians, but that he undertook journeys into other lands and there too similarly diffused useful arts. And in fact it was expressly stated that Osiris spread them not by the sword but by persuasion.

The story goes on to say that Osiris's brother Typhon wanted to institute new things in opposition to what had proved beneficial for the Egyptians over the centuries through the influence of Osiris. Typhon wanted to inaugurate all sorts of novelties, or, as we would say today, after the institutions founded by Osiris had existed for hundreds of years, Typhon launched a revolution while Osiris was absent spreading his institutions among other peoples. This differs a little from the latest example of revolution, in which, whatever novelties were introduced, it was not done while the other side was absent, extending beneficent institutions among other nations. Anyway, between Osiris and Typhon, that is how it went. The myth proceeds:

Isis, who was Osiris's consort, and was waiting at home in Egypt, prevented Typhon's innovations from being really sweeping. That enraged Typhon, and when Osiris returned from his wanderings, Typhon slew him and got rid of the dead body. Isis had to search a long time for the corpse. She found it at last in Phoenicia, and brought it back home to Egypt. Typhon now became even angrier, and tore the dead body to pieces. Isis collected the pieces and out of each piece, by using spices and other arts, she made a being again, which had the complete form of Osiris. She then gave to the priests of the land a third of the whole territory of Egypt, so that Osiris's burial place should be kept a secret, but his service and worship performed with renewed vigor.

There is then a remarkable addition to this myth: Osiris came back from the underworld, after his worship had already been inaugurated in Egypt, and busied himself with the instruction of Horus, his son, whom Isis had borne after his death. Then it is told that Isis was imprudent enough to release Typhon, whom she had succeeded in imprisoning. Thereupon Horus, her son, became angry, tore the crown from her head and replaced it with cow's horns. Typhon was defeated in two battles with the assistance of Hermes (the Roman Mercury, Hermes for the Greeks). A kind of Horus cult, the cult of the son of Osiris and Isis, was instituted.

One way or another, the Greeks heard of these Egyptian stories of world mysteries. It is remarkable how often the Greeks spoke of the same being that was spoken of in Egypt, or in Phoenicia or Lydia, and so forth. These conceptions of the divinities flowed into one another, as it were, and this is very characteristic and significant. When the Greeks heard the name Osiris, they could picture something from it, they identified what the Egyptians understood under the name Osiris with something of which they too had certain concepts. Although the name was different, what the Egyptian conceived of as Osiris was not foreign to the Greek. Please, take note of this. It is very significant.

We find the whole thing once more in the *Germania* of Tacitus. There Tacitus described the gods that he found in the North a hundred years after the founding of Christianity, and he described them with Roman names. He gave Roman names to the gods whom he found there, despite the fact that these gods had of course other names. He recognized their being and could assign them Roman names. We find in the *Germania* that he knew that in the North people had a god that was the same god as Hercules, and so on. That is very significant and it points to something very deep and meaningful. It shows that in those ancient times, there was a certain common consciousness concerning spiritual things. The Greeks knew how to picture something as Osiris, independent of the name, because they had something similar. What was concealed behind the name Osiris was not unfamiliar to them.

We must keep this well in mind to recognize that despite the differences of separate myths, a certain community of soul existed. One wishes at times that there might be as much common understanding among modern human beings as, say, between the Greeks and the Egyptians, so that the Greeks understood what the Egyptians expressed. A Greek would never have uttered as much nonsense about Egyptian conceptions as Woodrow Wilson is able to think up in one week about European conceptions—if one can call it thinking! According to the Greeks, Chronos had begotten an illegitimate son by Rhea, and this irregularly begotten son was Osiris. So just think: the Greeks hear that the Egyptians have an Osiris, and the Greeks on their part relate that Osiris is the son of Chronos and Rhea, but not begotten in the right way; in fact the incorrectness of his conception was such that Helios the sun god, in his anger about the matter, made Rhea barren. Thus, on one hand, the Greeks find a certain relationship between their own conception of the gods and the Egyptian ones. But, on the other hand, what the Egyptians in a certain sense formed as their highest concept of a god, the Osiris concept, is, for the Greeks, connected with an irregular origin from the Titan race, from Chronos and Rhea.

We can get a first impression of this, albeit a surface impression, and we shall need to dig much deeper presently, if we are clear that the Egyptians sought to learn of the eternal part of the human soul. They sought to know that which traverses births and deaths, but in order to know of this eternal part in life they expressly turned the soul's gaze beyond death. To the people of Egypt, through whom the Greeks learned of Osiris, he is no longer the god of the living, but the god of the dead, the god who sits on the Throne of the World and passes judgment when the human being has gone through the gate of death, that is, the god whom humans have to meet after death. At the same time, however, the Egyptian knew that the same god who judges humans after death has at one time ruled over the living.

The moment one puts these ideas together, one is no longer as inclined to agree with Dupuis's verdict that it was only a matter of astronomical events. There is much to captivate our attention in Dupuis's judgments, but on closer inspection they reveal themselves as very superficial. I have said that the Egyptians, in the age when the Greeks received the Osiris concept from them, directed their mind above all to the human soul after death. This lay far from the Greek mind. To be sure, the Greeks too spoke of the human soul after death, but, inasmuch as they spoke of their gods, they did not really speak of the Osiris nature of such gods as primarily to sit in judgment after death. The race to which Zeus belonged was a race of gods for the living: Zeus, Hera, Pallas Athene, Mars, Apollo, and so on. Humans preferred to look up to this world when they turned their mind's eye to the world to which human beings belong between birth and death. But these gods were, so to say, the last divine race of the three successive generations of gods to which the Greeks turned their gaze.

As you know, the oldest generation of gods is connected to Uranus and Gaia, or better said; Gaia and Uranus. They were the earliest divine pair, together with all the siblings, and so on, who belonged to them. From this divine pair were descended the Titans, to whom Chronos and Rhea also belonged, and above all Oceanus. As you know, according to the myth Uranus had evoked the wrath of his spouse Gaia through certain cruel regulations, so she prevailed upon Chronos, their son, to make his father on the world throne impotent, and thus we see the old divine rulership replaced by the younger one, by Chronos and Rhea and all that belongs with them. You know too that in the Greek myth Chronos had the characteristic, somewhat unsavory in various respects, of swallowing all his children as soon as they were born, which was not pleasant for the mother, Rhea. (I am calling attention to various features which we shall particularly need.) And you know too that she saved Zeus and brought him up to overthrow Chronos, just as Chronos had overthrown Uranus, only in another way, so that once again a new race of gods arrives. And then we have Hera and Zeus, with all the brothers and sisters, and their children, and so on.

An important feature in the myth, which I must mention since we will need it if we wish to regard the myth as foundation for all sorts of world conceptions, is the following: Before he overcame the Titans and cast them into Tartarus, Zeus had prevailed on the goddess Metis, the goddess of cunning, to provide him with an emetic, so that all the children swallowed by Chronos could be brought again to the light of day. Thus Zeus could have his brothers and sisters again, for of course they had been in Chronos's body. Zeus alone had been rescued by his mother Rhea.

So we have three successive generations of gods: Gaia-Uranus; Uranus overthrown through Gaia, because of his cruelty, supplanted by the children Chronos and Rhea; then Chronos overthrown again through Zeus, likewise at the instigation of Rhea. In the Zeus circle we have the gods who meet us as actual Greek history makes its appearance.

Now I should like to call special attention to a very significant feature of this Greek mythology that is not stressed

clearly enough, despite its being one of the most important features. The macrocosm is ruled by the three successive races of gods. But while Gaia and Uranus, Rhea and
Chronos, Hera and Zeus are ruling, the human being,
according to the Greek conception, is already everywhere
in existence. Humanity is unquestionably there already.
Therefore, at a time when Chronos and Rhea had not yet
reigned, when the rulers were still Gaia and Uranus—but
then especially when Chronos reigned with Rhea, and
Zeus was not yet in possession of the emetic—according to
the Greeks there were already humans upon the earth.
And, what is more, as the Greeks told it, they lived a hap-
pier life than in later times. The later human beings are
descended from those earlier ones. In other words, the
Greek consciousness was the following: up above rules
Zeus, but we human beings descend from other forefathers who were not yet ruled by Zeus. This is an important
feature of Greek theology: the Greeks venerated their
Zeus, their Hera, their Pallas Athene, but were quite clear
that they had not been created by these gods, what one
would generally call "created," but that humans predated
by far the reign of these gods.

That this is especially important for the Greek gods can
strike you when you look at the matter from the point of
view of Jewish theology. It is, of course, quite unthinkable
to ascribe the same feature to the Jewish teaching. You
could not possibly imagine the Old Testament relating
human beings to ancestors who had not yet come under
the rulership of Yahweh and the Elohim. Thus we have
here something radically different in the Greek teachings
about the gods. The Greek looks up to the gods and
knows: they indeed are ruling now, but they have nothing
to do with what I call "creation" of the human race.

This was absolutely impossible within the Old Testament
conception. In the Old Testament those whom humanity

looked upon as gods were in the main far more concerned with the creation of the human being. In observing the course of world events, it is indispensable to consider such things. The point is not merely to form concepts, but to be able to form concepts that connect one with reality; the especially characteristic, the especially representative concepts, those are the ones we must have in mind.

And with this, we have considered an important feature of Greek mythology. Let us look at it some more. When the Greeks looked up to the gods, they did not have the consciousness that they had been created by these gods. For human beings were already there, as we have said, before these gods had assumed their rulership. What these gods were able to do was, for the Greeks, quite a respectable amount, but they could not produce a human race on a planet. In the Greek consciousness these gods could not produce a human race.

Now, what actually were the gods of the Zeus circle, the Olympian gods, for the Greek consciousness? To form even a historical concept of what these gods were—I mean now in the Greek consciousness, we have of course said various things about these gods, but let us place ourselves in the Greek consciousness—what were they? Well, they were not beings that would normally interact with humans. In fact they dwelt on Olympus, they dwelt in the clouds, and so on. They merely paid visits, sometimes sympathetic, and sometimes unsympathetic visits; Zeus in particular, as you know, sometimes paid sympathetic or unsympathetic visits to the human world. In certain respects the gods were useful; but they also did things about which modern people, who are somewhat more narrow-minded than the Greeks, would probably go to court and cite Zeus as a co-respondent in a divorce suit, and so on. In any case, these gods had a half-divine, half-human connection with humanity, and such beings, so it was thought, are not materialized in the flesh. When Zeus wanted to conduct his affairs he assumed all sorts of guises, didn't he?—a swan, golden rain, and so on. Thus in ordinary life these gods were not incarnated in the flesh. But on the other hand, if we look deeper, we find that the Greeks had the consciousness that these gods were connected with humans who lived in primeval times. Far more than looking up to the connection with the stars, as Dupuis supposed, the Greeks looked up to primeval human beings and established a connection between the concept of a Zeus being/nature—please note exactly how I form the sentence, for that is the point—and some ancient ruler of a long-past age. Please note that I have not said that the Greeks had the idea that what they meant by Zeus had been an ancient ruler; instead I said: that which they pictured as Zeus, they *associated* with an ancient ruler who had lived in long bygone ages. For the kind of connection with Zeus or for that matter with other gods was a somewhat complicated one.

Let us look more closely at the words, so that we can form an idea of what really underlies them. Let us suppose that at some time a personality had lived in Thrace, a region in northern Greece, on whom the Zeus concept was fastened. Now the Greek, even the quite ordinary Greek was quite clear: I do not, as it were, venerate this ancestor, nor do I venerate the single individuality which has lived in this ancestor; nevertheless I venerate something which had some connection with this ancient forefather, this ancient king of Thrace, or of Epirus. The Greek had in fact this idea: there was once such a king in whose whole being not only his own individuality lived, but the individuality of a supersensible being; this had expressed itself, had lived upon the earth, by descending into a human being. The Zeus concept was not made earthly in this way; it was rather brought into connection with an ancient ruler, who at one time had furnished the garment—or let us say the dwelling place—for this Zeus being. Thus the Greek differentiated essentially that which he conceived of as Zeus from the human individuality who had lived in the body to which the Zeus concept was referred. But the Zeus rulership, the rule of Zeus and the gods, took its starting point, as it were, from the fact that Zeus had descended, had lived in a human being, had found his center there in order to work in the being of humanity—but then went on working, no longer as an ordinary human but in fact as an "Olympian." And it was the same in the case of the other Greek gods.

Why did the Greeks form this conception that there was once a ruler who was "possessed" by Zeus, but that now there is no longer a ruler who can be possessed by Zeus, and Zeus only rules as a supersensible being? Because the Greeks knew that human evolution had progressed, that it had changed. In other words, the Greeks knew that there were ancient times when human beings could have Imaginations in a particularly outstanding degree. A certain clairvoyance naturally remained for some few, but the authority of the Imaginations had disappeared: the beings who can still have real Imaginations can hold sway only in supersensible realms, for the course of human life between birth and death.

This is the essence of what the Greeks pictured to themselves concerning their gods: they are beings who can *imagine.* But the time is past when these beings who can imagine could enter into human bodies. For human bodies are no longer adapted to Imaginations. We are governed by a race of beings who can have Imaginations, while we no longer can have them. The Greeks had a quite unsentimental concept of their gods. In any case it would have been rather difficult to be sentimental about Zeus. Yet the Greeks said to themselves in the quiet of their hearts (I shall again elaborate the matter somewhat, one must add detail when one wants to be quite clear): "We humans are going through a definite evolution; we have developed from atavistic clairvoyance to Intuition, Inspiration, Imagination; now we must have ordinary objective thinking. But the gods have not ventured there. They have remained in their imaginative consciousness; otherwise they would have to be humans and wander on earth in the flesh. It did not suit them (so thought the Greeks in their unsentimental way of regarding the gods) to pass over to objective thinking, so they have not descended to the earth, but kept to their imaginative consciousness. In this way, however, they rule over us, for they have more power, as it were, since the imaginative concept, when utilized fully, is more powerful than the objective concept."

From this, however, you see that the Greeks looked back to a time when humans' formation of concepts, their observation and perception were different, and this retrospective look went hand in hand with the ideas they formed of the gods. Thus they looked back to Zeus and Hera, and said: They are ruling over us now; at one time we were like them, but we have developed further and have become weaker in the process. Therefore they can rule us, they have remained in the condition prevalent at that time. The Greeks ascribed to their gods what we today would call a certain luciferic quality. And those beings who had remained at the Imagination stage—this was elaborated in the Greek consciousness—were themselves the successors of the beings who remained at the Inspiration stage. Hera and Zeus stopped at Imagination, Rhea and Chronos at Inspiration, Gaia and Uranus at Intuition.

You see, the Greeks examined their own soul, and they connected their genealogies of the gods with the evolution of humanity and the different states of consciousness. This connection was felt, it was perceived. The eldest gods, Gaia and Uranus, were beings whose whole inner relation to the world was shaped by the fact that they had an intuitive consciousness. They wanted to remain at the stage of Intuition; and those at the stage of Inspiration rose up against them. And again the Inspired Ones wished to stay with Inspiration; and those living in the imaginative consciousness set themselves against them. The Inspired Ones were overcome by the Imagining Ones. We live as human beings and above us stand the Imagining Ones. Now you know that in the Prometheus myth, the Greeks already expressed the desire for a weapon in their struggle against the Imagining Ones.

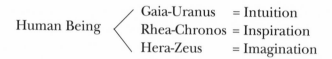

The Greeks arranged their divinities in chronological layers expressive of the way they looked back to earlier stages of consciousness of the essence that was, in parallel fashion, evolving as humanity. The Greeks made clear that, in their mind, this was connected with their retrospective look upon the gods. Just think how deeply significant this is for our understanding of the Greek consciousness! Looking back to the generations of the gods, the Greeks looked back to the past in their own mental life. They connected the ancient intuitive beings with Gaia, the earth, and Uranus, the heavens, and connected the inspirational gods with Rhea and Chronos. In the case of Gaia and Uranus we can still perceive what they were. Rhea and Chronos, on the other hand, are described as Titans. What are they actually?

Now for some centuries, humanity has lost practically all consciousness of what lies at the foundation of all this. But let me remind you that a few hundred years ago, in the Middle Ages, the human being was brought into connection with three fundamental elements: Salt, Mercury, and Sulphur. You can still find this knowledge in Jacob Boehme and Paracelsus, even as late as Saint-Martin's time. Jacob Boehme still makes the following notation: Sal = Salt; Mercur = Quicksilver; Sulphus = Sulphur.

What was understood by this was not identical but yet was related to the Greeks' meaning when they spoke of Gaia-Uranus; Rhea-Chronos; Hera-Zeus. For you see, Chronos drove Uranus from world rulership, and Gaia became for practical purposes a widow. What happened to her after that? She became what is "Earth"—not the ordinary earth which we find outside, but the earth that human beings carry in themselves, i.e., salt. If humans could make conscious use of the salt within them, then they would have Intuition, as the investigator of nature in the Middle Ages knew. So a process which had still been alive in the old Gaia-Uranus time has sunk into the deep recesses of human nature.

A more recent process which has also sunk deep into human nature can be described as the Rhea-Chronos process. The Greeks said that the power of Rhea was once widespread, and "Chronos" represented the forces that confronted Rhea. Chronos was overthrown. What has been left? Well, just as from Uranus-Gaia the dead salt has been left, so from Chronos-Rhea the fluid mercury has been left; the fluid in humans that can take a drop formation has been left behind. But humans cannot make conscious use of that either; it has sunk into unconscious depths.

This, of course, was a very, very long time ago, and in the time of the Greeks it was already gone by, for the Greeks said to themselves: Zeus's time upon earth was in the long ago primeval ages, but at that time humans could make use of the sulphur to be found in them. If humans could consciously use their salt, they would be able to use Intuition in an atavistic way. If they could consciously use mercury, the fluid element, they would be able to use Inspiration, and Imagination if they could use sulphur— not in the altered sense that has come to us through successive transmissions, but in the actual sense that the alchemists of the Middle Ages still understood it when they spoke of the "philosophical sulphur." Today there is also a philosophical sulphur: professors of philosophy manufacture vast quantities of sulfurous hot air, but it is not quite what the alchemists had in mind. They were referring to an imaginative consciousness, an atavistic Imagining, which was connected with the use of this active sulphur in humans. The Greeks and the priests of their Mysteries (for the mysteries of salt, mercury, and sulphur are ancient) also said that human beings, through their evolution, have overcome the atavism that would allow them to make an atavistic use of sulphur. But Zeus and his circle have withdrawn into the supersensible realm and avail themselves of the sulphur processes; hence Zeus can hurl his lightning. If, like Zeus, human beings could hurl lightning, that is, transform the sulphur through Imagination into reality, if they could inwardly and consciously hurl lightning, then they would use Imagination atavistically. That is what the Greeks wished to say when they said that Zeus could hurl lightning.

As late as Saint-Martin, the sulphur of the alchemists was known to have meant something different from the ordinary earthly sulphur, which could at most be said—excuse the plain speaking—to be the excrement of what was understood by Saint-Martin and the philosophers before him as the real sulphur, which they also called the "philosophical sulphur." And Saint-Martin still speaks of thunder and lightning's real connection with the processes of the macrocosmic, or one could say the cosmic, sulphur. Today, many of the physical, natural scientific explanations that creep into science have a touch of brimstone in them, but this is not exactly a "philosophical sulphur." Of course, the really clever people of today are far beyond talking of sulphur processes in the cosmos when thunder and lightning arise, for lightning and thunder arise, as any elementary physics book will tell you, through some sort of friction processes in the clouds. Not that it is possible to find anything really logical in what is said about lightning and thunder: Wet clouds in their mutual action are supposed to create the electricity which comes about through thunder and lightning, but if an electrical experiment is made in the schoolroom, each piece of apparatus is most carefully dried because the least dampness prevents any electricity from arising. It would seem then that the clouds up there are not wet after all! The same teacher who can do nothing with a damp, or even not completely bone-dry, electric machine will at the same time explain that wet clouds are supposed to be connected with the creation of electricity. It certainly gets mixed-up, doesn't it? I wanted only to say that in Saint-Martin we still find a consciousness that this element of which the Greeks dreamt when they spoke of Hera and Zeus, had something to do with lightning and thunder.

The way it is, even superficial ideas can indicate to us that certain natural processes, the salt, mercury, and sulphur-processes as they were conveyed in earlier times, are linked with what the Greeks possessed in their mythology. Let us not lose sight of this basic fact. We need such fundamental concepts in order to make the right transition to our own time.

Thus the Greeks looked back to generations of gods, to conditions that had ceased to exist but that had been perceptible to earlier ages of humanity. They connected what lived in their gods with what we call natural processes. Mythology was therefore at the same time a sort of natural science. And the more one learns to know mythology, the deeper the natural science to be found in it, only a different natural science, one which is at the same time a science of the soul. This is how the Greeks thought, and how the Egyptians, too, conceived of their Osiris, who once had ruled but now was in the underworld.

Do you notice how different the things are and yet how they can all be traced back to a common type? Whereas the Greeks refer to earlier ages when a being like Zeus, who in their own time could live only supersensibly, could actually assume a human form, so too the Egyptians could point to an older age when Osiris or many Osirises—the number is irrelevant—ruled, an age when the gods descended into human beings, when they were present. But that time has passed, and the Egyptians could no longer find Osiris by looking to a human being on the physical plane, they had to look to the world which human beings enter when they go through the portal of death. Thus the Egyptians too harked back to an earlier stage in the evolution of human consciousness when they distinguished between the Osiris who could once wander the earth and the Osiris who can now no longer wander the earth, who belongs solely to the kingdom of death.

We confine ourselves today to the two mythologies and tomorrow will touch briefly upon the Old Testament teachings before we draw any conclusions. But we can make the following statement: The Greek and Egyptian consciousness of their gods expressed a remembrance of the ancient times of atavistic clairvoyance; the gods have vanished, they are no longer here. The descriptions of the destinies which human beings once shared with the gods, whether with Zeus or Chronos in Greece, or with Osiris in Egypt, expressed this other knowledge: looking farther back, the relationship of human beings to the macro-cosm was different from what it is now. This relationship has altered.

Looking back in this way to earlier ages when the gods walked among humans had a distinct reality for these ancient peoples, since they knew that humans in these ages stood as microcosm to macrocosm in a way different than in their own time. The old atavistic clairvoyance actually faded away in the fourth post-Atlantean epoch. This is what Greek mythology sought to express, as did the Egyptian Osiris mythology.

5 January 1918

YESTERDAY I endeavored to show how the special configuration of mythologies such as the Osiris myth, Greek
mythology—and in a certain sense even the Old Testament
teachings to which we will return presently—is associated
with changes in the states of human consciousness. We
know how things stand in respect to the evolution of
human consciousness; we know that we have to take into
consideration earlier times of human evolution in which
an old clairvoyance existed, an ability to perceive super-
earthly things. We may want to look back at these things,
for this retrospective helps us orient ourselves. Humanity
must regain a vision directed to the supersensible; it will be
found again by following the path of spiritual science,
through spiritual scientific thinking. The resolve to orien-
tate ourselves toward things yet to come through a consideration of what has been will help us see what each person
can do, no matter where he or she stands in the world.

For in a certain sense, things that take place in later
times are connected with events of earlier times. From the
vantage point of our fifth post-Atlantean epoch, which is
still unfolding around us, we are looking back to the
fourth post-Atlantean, or Greco-Latin, epoch and to the
third, or Egyptian, epoch; the latter was already a time
in which it was natural for humans to express in certain

mythical pictures and imaginations what they thought and felt about cosmic mysteries. We have already stated in another connection that we of the fifth post-Atlantean epoch have to recapitulate in a sort of inverted way what happened in the third, the Egypto-Chaldean epoch, so that it emerges again in a different form. And by the way, the book *The Spiritual Guidance of the Individual and Humanity* also refers to this subject.

We saw yesterday that in the time of the Greco-Latin evolution, beginning with the seventh or eighth century before our era, there was a kind of looking back on the part of humanity, and that looking back to other states of consciousness was in fact expressed in imaginative myths about the ruling spiritual beings. In the fourth epoch, people knew: when we look around us, we see only the physical world, but we can reflect on the other worlds. Moreover, if you have followed attentively what I say in my book *The Riddles of Philosophy*, you know that in Greek times, and even much later, people *saw* Ideas, as it were, as Goethe still did, and that they could really say: we see them. Entirely abstract thinking has only appeared in the modern age. But at that time, there was indeed a seeing of ideas, a seeing of spiritual realities, a living in spiritual realities.

In the fourth post-Atlantean epoch this was no longer the case in the full sense, but people remembered that it had been so earlier. They said—and in fact this was the truth—that there were beings who lived in supersensible worlds and still preserved life in the imaginative consciousness. For the Greeks, the individuals of the Zeus circle were such beings.

And the Egyptians said to themselves: When Osiris wandered upon earth, people still lived directly with Imaginations. The Egyptians did not, of course, mean *one specific* Osiris, but they did believe there had been a time when human beings on earth lived in Imaginations. And one described the type of human soul which was able to live in Imaginations by saying: Osiris lived upon earth. This living in Imaginations was lost and slain. Osiris was killed by his brother Typhon—that is, by that force of the human soul which to be sure is still turned to the supersensible realm, but is no longer willing to develop the imaginative faculties. The ancient clairvoyance exists no more. The forces active in the old clairvoyance are now amidst the dead. That is why Osiris is the judge of the dead; the human being meets him after passing through the gate of death. The figures of Osiris and Isis were associated with the death mystery by those people who set the Osiris myth at the center of their thought. Everything that I have said can be found in the details through which the Osiris myth has been elaborated. Among other things, the point of time is specified when, according to the legend, Osiris was killed by Typhon.

And just as we can point to a very specific heavenly constellation that the Magi of the East knew to be the constellation in which the new cosmic age was to approach (we have pointed out in the Christmas lectures that by a certain constellation of the "Virgin," the Magi of the East knew that they were to bring their offerings to the new World Saviour), so, too, those whose thoughts centered on the Osiris myth looked back to very definite star constellations. They said that Osiris was slain, by which they meant: the old life in the Imaginations vanished when the setting sun in autumn stood at seventeen degrees of Scorpio and, in the opposite point of the heavens, the full moon rose in Taurus, or in the Pleiades. The followers of Osiris declared this definite point of the year marked by the full moon rising in Taurus, as the time when Osiris vanished from the earth, that is, when he was no longer present there. Of course, the way these things happen, they leave legacies. There have always been people, stragglers even up to recent centuries, who possessed imaginative clairvoyance, but the point is to indicate when imaginative clairvoyance disappeared from earth as a normal faculty of the human soul. And people were aware that in the age when imaginative clairvoyance prevailed on, earth conditions were quite different from what they were later. And this too was plainly indicated in the Osiris-Isis myth. But these are precisely the things for which the commentators of the Isis and Osiris myth show so little understanding.

As you know, it is said that when Isis discovered that her husband Osiris had been slain, she departed on a search for the dead body. She found it at last in Byblos in Phoenicia and brought the corpse from Phoenicia back to Egypt. Such a myth expresses a deep wisdom, a wisdom about human physiology. What were conditions like during the time of Osiris? During this time there was not yet a script of the kind that was developed later. What prevailed in Egypt during the age of Osiris was picture writing and it was considered sacred. And how actually was picture writing brought about? It was brought about by taking the most important signs, not from animal or other earthly forms, but from the star constellations, in fact from the things clairvoyance saw in the star constellations. To make a comparison with something that has been in our minds lately, I might say: You have heard how Olaf Åsteson in the "Dream of Olaf Åsteson" experiences the spirit snake, the spirit dog, and the spirit bull; he describes what he feels about them. Imagine such pictures, but in a far more perfect form, as signs—these signs, then, are images of Imaginations. Signs like the signs of the earliest writing were held to be holy. In ancient times, cosmic wisdom was contained in such signs, wisdom which was at the same time a wisdom of the celestial sky, inasmuch as people read the cosmic mysteries in the star script, as only the dead can do now. The gift of possessing a writing which is really a reproduction of Imaginations, belonged to humanity only at a certain period of time, and then vanished. And the ancients knew that this imaginative way of writing existed in the age of Osiris. Together with the dying away of the old life of the world in Imaginations, the ancient picture script disappeared and what has become the abstract script arose. This no longer expresses mysteries, but gradually, since it has become abstract, has come to express only the sense world—becoming the ordinary alphabet script. Just as, in those ancient times, Osiris was looked upon as the hero, the divine hero of the imaginative script, so Typhon, his brother and opponent, was the hero of the abstract alphabetic script that evolved from it.

This is also indicated profoundly in the Osiris-Isis myth. Isis must travel to Phoenicia to find the corpse of Osiris, that is, to find the picture script transformed into letter script. The letter script was "found," invented as we say, in Phoenicia. Whereas the Egyptians in their old mysteries in the time of Osiris had a picture writing reflecting Imaginations, the abstract script has now come from Phoenicia back to Egypt. Thus the transition from the old concrete conception in the imaginative script to the newer concept in the abstract script also found an expression in the Osiris-Isis myth.

All these things lie in the course of human evolution. We are looking back to an older experience in Imaginations. Real physiological wisdom is, in fact, expressed in the myths. Thinking gradually passed over to abstractions—not immediately to the quite empty abstractions of today but to the somewhat fuller abstractions of about the sixth and fifth centuries B.C., for example, in the work of Thales, whose name is generally placed at the beginning of the history of philosophy. (You can look it up in my *Riddles of Philosophy*.)

You can see from this that humanity has to look back to earlier evolutionary periods from the vantage point of very different soul conditions. To be sure, certain modern secret societies know about these entirely different conditions, but they hold that such things should still be kept under lock and key. That is not true for the present day, although it is a little dangerous to talk of these things past a certain point. Up to that point, however, it is not just a case of *should*; these things *must* be spoken of today, because the knowledge of ancient conditions of human consciousness helps us orient ourselves for what is to develop as the new consciousness. If we have the knowledge of what once existed, it can help us bring about the necessary new conditions for evolution, although they are of an entirely different kind from those required earlier.

These days, you find that boys go through a change of voice at puberty. As we know, it is the expression of an organic process, which occurs differently in the female sex, and which to outward appearances makes greater inroads into the female human being, since the process reaches more directly into the physical body. But that is not true. The influence on boys is just as strong, though it lies in a different sphere, so to say, and comes to external physical expression only in the change of voice.

This attainment of maturity by the human being is, and in fact has been ever since Osiris died for the outer world, almost entirely a physical process. When Osiris lived, it was not merely a physical process, but a soul process as well. The boy of fourteen or fifteen years (as you know, we have already spoken of other experiences at the time of puberty) experienced not only that his voice changed; that which presently only enters, presses into, the region of the voice, extending from the sexual essences of the organism, in those ancient times also affected directly the thoughts, the conceptual world of the young boy. We must deal with

such things truthfully; the voice apparatus is simply pervaded with the sexual essences of the organism. Today the
voice "breaks" or mutates; in those days the thoughts
mutated too, since it was still the ancient imaginative time.
In those times the young boy before the age of puberty had
certain Imaginations; it was a living process and all knew
that the child up to nine or ten years of age had Imaginations—Imaginations of spiritual events in the atmosphere.
(To this day there are still slight remains of this in almost
every child of a tender age, only people pay no attention to
it, or talk the children out of it as being foolish nonsense.)
Spiritual events are taking place around us in the air all the
time. The air is not only what physical science describes,
but the locus of spiritual events. These spiritual events,
essentially events of the etheric world, were perceived by
children in full Imaginations up to the time of puberty.
And when puberty arrived—not only for the voice, but also
for the life of concepts—human beings felt something in
themselves (it was in fact that which shot up out of the
forces which are usually called in physiology the sex
forces), something of which they said: What I saw as a child
through the Imagination in the atmosphere, now comes to
life in me again; it is a perception, it lives in me. That did
indeed happen. Human beings were aware that they had
taken something into themselves out of the atmosphere.
Formerly the young boy had seen it outside; now he felt it
within himself.

For girls too, in those ancient times, there had been,
before puberty, a perception in Imaginations of what was
outside in the atmosphere. But after puberty that which, in
the case of the boy, merely emerged as the feeling of an
alteration in the mental life, in the case of the girl, felt like
an ascent of still more inward Imaginations: it was the
human image that she would perceive within herself again
and again in Imagination. And then she would tell herself:

What I now perceive imaginatively is the same as I experienced as a prepubescent child, out in cosmic space, as imaginative pictures. Each in its own way, the two sexes experienced deep in the soul that they knew: something is born in me, which cosmic space has fructified in me.

Thus we have a still more concrete form of the Osiris-Isis myth: it is universal wisdom insofar as it is won from the atmosphere, but it has an organic connection with the deeper layers of the human spirit. Try and get a better idea of it from the following: Humans presently think in an abstract way, inasmuch as they long to know through the head the lawfulness of the world. In ancient times human beings were clear that it is impossible to know truly this way, merely through head knowledge, but that we know through our whole being. We know what goes on outside in space, what goes on etherically, by first perceiving it as it were externally, and then, after puberty, picturing or feeling it inwardly. How then do you perceive today, with the abstract perception that you have? You discover something which you see with the senses; then you think it over afterwards. The two steps follow each other in rapid succession. With the mysteries, through which humans beings in ancient times penetrated into the laws of the atmosphere as represented in Imaginations, it was a different matter. Throughout childhood, up to puberty, humans perceived, they only perceived; later in life, they worked it over inwardly. In a way, it is only the succession of a perceptive process and a thinking process spread out in time; whereas today, when to observe abstractly and when to reflect, when to form abstract concepts, is left to the individual's own discretion. What we now crowd into a few moments regarding the outer physical world used to be spread over the whole life. To perceive, to conceive, was something which humans, in their relation to the world, thought of as spread out over the whole of human life between birth and death. Up to the age of puberty they perceived certain things, afterwards they reflected upon them. This is the way it used to be.

But now think, people said to themselves: This perceiving and reflecting are connected in a certain way with the day, with the rising and setting sun. With the rising sun, one wakes, gets up, begins to perceive and to think; with the setting sun this ceases, since one lies down to sleep. Thus people connected perceiving and thinking with the day; and what was spread out over the course of life between birth and death, they brought into connection with more widely extended cosmic events in the heavens. Just as my thinking and perceiving depends on the sun, on the ordinary rising and setting of the sun, in the same way whatever humans develop in the way of perceptions and thoughts depends on larger, far-flung star constellations that reappear after centuries, after millennia. And just as, in the past, people connected ordinary perception and thinking with the day, with sunrise and sunset—indeed as people do today though they don't think so and even may believe they go by the clock— so they connected matters concerning more comprehensive cosmic mysteries with the other star constellations, with the other events in the heavens.

You see, a deep logic, a deep wisdom lies in these things. Superficialities like Dupuis's explanations will not let us get at the facts. But something else too is bound up with it. These ancient peoples, and we could speak of others besides the Egyptians and the Greeks, knew that the more inward-lying forces of human nature are connected with what comes to expression in celestial happenings, in the constellations. That decadence which is expressed in current attitudes to the sex problem, and the most current attitude is the most decadent of all, was totally foreign to those ancient peoples. For them it was something very different. They had the feeling that when the voice broke, the thoughts "broke" too, and when these things happened, the sexual essences were suffused throughout the human being. It was their deep conviction that the divine was then pouring itself forth in the human being. Hence we find in all old religious rituals things which these days are viewed only in a prurient sense: the sexual symbols, the so-called sexual symbols (phallic symbols), point thus to this connection between the atmosphere with its air events and the human processes of knowledge which take place during the whole of human life between birth and death.

"Through my eye, through my ear," said these people, "I am connected with what is brought by the day. Through the deeper, more inward-lying forces, I am connected with something quite different, with the secrets of the air, which, however, are perceived only in imaginative experience." And this imaginative experience in its concrete form, I have described for you with reference to these early times.

The Old Testament conception of these matters was different inasmuch as it put doctrine in the place of actual experience. The Egyptian of the Osiris age, especially of the earlier Osiris age, said: "The true human being only enters me with puberty, for I then take in what formerly I saw in Imaginations. The air transmits to me the true human being." In the doctrine of the Old Testament this was transformed into the following conception: The Elohim or Yahweh have breathed into the human being the living breath (*Odem*), the air. Here the essence was lifted out of the direct living experience and became doctrine, theory. This was necessary, for—and this is the meaning of the Old Testament—only so could human beings be led from that symbiosis with the outer world, in which an inner connection still existed between the human microcosm and the macrocosm, the world, to their further evolution (of which I will speak later). As the connection gradually vanished, it became necessary to fall back on just such a doctrine as the Old Testament.

But now came the time of the death of Osiris—and therewith the time too in which, while one thing became finer, the other thing, as it were, became coarser. How is that to be understood? Well, you can imagine it thus: Reverting to the old Osiris time, the human being before puberty saw or felt the light Imaginations in the outer air. I am talking only of the male sex here.

Up to the time of puberty, the boy saw the light Imaginations in the air in his environment. Afterwards he had the feeling that they had entered into him, and the changes occurred of which we have spoken. For the child, the air was everywhere filled with light phenomena; for the grown man, the matured man, the air was still there of course, but he knew that as a child he had seen something else in it. He knew that the air was at the same time the bearer, the mother, of light. He knew that it was not true that when he looked out into the air there was nothing in it but what was shown physically. Beings lived in it which were to be perceived in Imagination.

For the Greeks these beings were *the beings of Zeus's circle.* Thus humans knew that there were beings in the air. But the fact that human states of consciousness have changed is connected with the fact that even objective things became different in their finer substantiality. Naturally, for the modern intellectual it is an outrage to say such things. I know it is an outrage, but it is nevertheless true: the air has become different. Naturally it has not changed in a way that can be tested by chemical reagents; nevertheless the air has become different. The air has lost its power to express the light Imaginations; the air has, one could say, become coarser. It has actually become different on earth since that ancient time. The air has become coarser. But not only the air; the human being too has become coarser.

That which formerly lived spiritually in the essences per-
meating the larynx and the rest of the organism has grown
coarser also. So in fact when we speak today of the sexual
essences we speak of something different from what one
would have spoken of in ancient times. Everyone in
ancient times knew: My day-to-day perceptions are connected with my personality; the rest, which I experience
from the atmosphere, experience with my whole life, that,
however, is connected with humanity as a whole, that goes
beyond the individual person. Hence they also sought to
fathom the social mysteries under which humans live
together, through the link which bound them with the
macrocosm; they looked for social wisdom in star wisdom.
But what lived in human beings as social wisdom bound
them in fact to the celestial. This was expressed in the most
commonplace concepts. A human couple before the death
of Osiris would never have felt anything other than that
they had received a child from heaven. That was a living
consciousness and it corresponded also with truth. And
this living consciousness could develop because humans
knew that whatever they experienced, they received out of
the air-filled space.

Of all this only the coarse dregs, so to say, have been left.
Just as in the air only the coarse sediment of those vigorous
forces of the air that previously revealed themselves in
Imaginations remains, so in the human being only the
coarse dregs are left behind. This needed to happen, since
otherwise humans could not have attained freedom and a
full consciousness of the ego. But still we are left with the
dregs. In this way, however, all that the ancients meant by
the divine, which as you can now readily realize was associated in a roundabout way with the sexual essences, all this
has been coarsened, not only the idea but also the reality.
Nevertheless, it is still there one way and another. Human
reproduction in those ancient times was thought to be in

direct connection with the micro-macrocosmic bond of humanity, as you have seen, but the whole of human social life on earth was in fact also thought to be associated with this micro-macrocosmic bond. Numa Pompilius went to the nymph Egeria to receive information from her as to how he should arrange social conditions in the Roman Empire. This, however, means nothing else than that he had let the star wisdom be imparted to him, had let the star-wisdom tell him how society should be organized. That which humans reproduce on earth, and which is connected with successive generations, was to be placed in the service of the stars' message. Just as individuals directed their life with their ordinary perceiving and thinking, according to the rising and setting of the sun, so too, what later became known as "nation-states," that is, human groups, were to be placed under the star constellations as expressions of cosmic relationships.

In German—and languages often contain memories of old conditions—we still have a remembrance of this connection in the fact that the relation of male and female is described by the word *Geschlecht* (sex) and the successive generations as *Geschlechter* (races). It is one and the same word: the *Geschlecht*, the family, interconnected blood relations, and then the relation of man and woman. This occurs also in other languages, and it always points to humanity's search for a recognizable connection between the macrocosm and what lies in their nature, in the deeper strata of their being.

These things have become coarsened in the way we have discussed. Among other remnants is the greedy and sentimental attachment to nationality, the clinging to the national, the chauvinistic impulse for the national; that is the lingering relic of what in the past could be thought of in very different contexts. But it is necessary to see through those things in order to know the truth contained in them.

What is expressed by the nationalistic longing? When a person develops to excess this national feeling, this sentiment for the nation, what is it that lives in it? Exactly the same as what lives in sexuality; sexual relations on one hand, and national sentiment on the other express in different forms the same reality. It is the sexual human being that lives through these two different poles. Being chauvinistic is nothing else really than developing a sort of group sexuality. One could say that where the sexual essences, or what is left of them, hold humans more firmly in their grip, there more national chauvinism is present, for it is the very force living in reproduction that comes to manifestation in national sentiment. Hence the battle-cry of the so-called "National Freedom," or "Peoples' Freedom," can only be understood in its more intimate dimensions if one calls it, without the least prurient meaning, "The Call for the Restoration of the Nations in the Light of the Sex Problem." It seems to me that the greatest mystery of the impulse of our time is the fact that these days the sexual problem is proclaimed in a very special form all over the earth, without people having any idea that, out of their subconscious, sexuality clothes itself in the words "Freedom of the Peoples." And sexual impulses play a much greater role in the catastrophic events of today, much, much greater than people imagine! For the roots of what is happening today lie, in fact, very deep.

Such truths must no longer be kept under lock and key in our present age. Certain secret societies have been able to keep them under lock and key, insofar as they have excluded women, in the strictest sense of the word. While even today joint work with women can lead to all sorts of problems, as has repeatedly been observed, yet the time has come in which right views on these matters must be spread among humanity. Of course all kinds of prurient, foolish, silly ideas have been spread abroad from certain directions, so that without any knowledge of the more intimate connections, all sorts of things are treated today as sexual problems. You can see how what here is pure, genuine, honorable truth comes in contact, on the one hand, with what can be the most impure, lowest way of thinking, as is shown from time to time in the outgrowths of psychoanalysis or similar things. You will always find, however, that whereas something rightly understood is profound truth, it needs hardly to be altered at all in words, but only to be permeated with a low-minded type of thought, to be reduced to a pernicious, stupid, thoroughly objectionable conception.

A former age could speak of "nations," when "nations" were pictured in such a way that one nation had its guardian spirit in Orion, another in another star, and one knew that one's life was ruled by the star constellations. One then appealed, as it were, to the heavenly order. Today when this heavenly ordering is no longer available, the appeal is a chauvinistic appeal to the merely national, that is, the assertion of an eminently psychosexual impulse, a backward luciferic impulse.

If one would see clearly and plainly what *is* today, one must not shrink from the actual underlying truth. But one can also see from such things why people are so afraid of the truth. Just imagine if, in the outcry on the freedom of nations and so forth that is raised today, people were to hear that "it all stems from sexual impulses"! Just imagine that! Imagine the crowing cock—I don't mean a particular one, not necessarily just Clemenceau; just picture all the declaimers on this theme, and imagine that they had to realize that their crow is nothing more after all than the mating call of the cock, however finely it is decked out in national garments!

These are things which humans must learn to know today and which they do not want to hear, for, as you know, things that are black are asserted to be white, and those that are white, black. The point is, that the ancient time of which I have spoken has brought us to the fifth post-Atlantean epoch, in which abstraction has gradually developed. At the boundary between the fourth and fifth post-Atlantean epochs, human beings, the best of them included, fought and killed each other over the intellectual value of abstraction. You can read about it in my *Riddles of Philosophy*, where I speak of the nominalism and realism of the Middle Ages. Abstraction had grown to such a pitch that people asked themselves: When I form a concept, has that any significance for the things outside, or is it only a name in my head? Today people no longer reflect on such things. Of what interest is it to people to know that human beings tormented themselves in the Middle Ages, when the abstractive power of thought was felt, about what role the so-called universals, the general ideas, play in the world! That one wrestled and strove about what role abstractions play! Nowadays no one thinks about this any more; people have already become used to abstractions. No one strives to get beyond the abstract impulse but, on the contrary, only to get thoroughly within it. The conflict over "universals" ultimately came to the point where it was said: "Universals, General Ideas, exist at first as specific Ideas in God: those are Universals *ante rem*; then the Ideas are in the objects: Universals *in rem*; and then the Ideas are in our mind, our soul: Universals *post rem*." That was an expedient, a way to find one's proper stand on the question: Are human beings connected with reality when they think, when they only think ideas? Something of how in ancient times human beings had been connected with reality could still be felt. In the past when human beings reached maturity they thought over, as it were, what as children they had formerly perceived; only then did they know that the true human being had entered. So in the Middle Ages one had to struggle desperately over the universals, over whether, when one thinks, something of reality is still left in one's thought or whether thought is entirely divorced from reality and has nothing to do with it. Since that time people have grown accustomed to take the universals, the abstractions, as abstractions, and are more or less completely cut off from reality in their consciousness.

Such a process is taking place continually on a small scale. Think for a moment: Words, which stand for concepts, are originally in direct connection with what is seen. For instance, a small group of fighting men has one man at the head, one man before the others; they call him the foremost, the first, *Furst* (Chief, Prince). The word was at first linked directly with what was beheld. Later, it was set free, it became a word which denoted something without any sort of connection with a direct perception. Just think to how many words this applies! And the next step is that certain words then become privileged, that speech becomes monopolized, becomes the property of the State. Even in language, certain things are developing in this direction, are they not? Take the simple case that someone has learned a great deal, has become wise; let us say, without trying to be funny, he is a learned man. In a certain naive way one might call him "Doctor." Here we have a connection with fact if we call someone "Doctor" who is seen to be learned. For this title still has a certain significance, when documentary evidence is provided by a corporation which gives this recognition. But the word loses its significance when it is monopolized, yet humankind is enthusiastic about such monopolizing nowadays. All possible words are to be monopolized. A person is not supposed merely through his gifts to be an "engineer," but this must also become a recognized title from heaven knows where. And increasingly things are to be loosed from their connections. This is a small example of the abstraction process, but it is accomplished wholesale with momentous effects. A family has a father. What is the connection between the *pater*, who is the father of the family, and the *Pater*, who is a priest? I wanted to bring this tearing loose of what is contained in the word forward because it illustrates the abstraction process taking place in humanity.

In the case of ideas it is much more mischievous than in language; people often make use of concepts without having the least idea of their connection with what is perceived. And when occasionally people search for the real observation behind the word, the results can be comical, frightfully comical! Just observe, there are whole libraries today about the sign of the cross, which is really a universal sign, spread over the world. Most amusing is all the learnedness applied to it!

This sign is traced back to this;

That was supposed to have been the cross of former times.

Sometimes writers trace that further back by saying that only the parts have been left, the swastika, and so on.

Yes, what has been written about it is frightfully clever, quite immensely clever, the way "cleverness" has been applied. I do not wish at all to go in for detailed criticism, but to tell the truth, cleverness is not enough. It should be obvious that the sign of the cross means nothing else than that the *human being* takes its stand, stretches out its arms and then is the cross. From above downwards goes a stream of existence that binds the person with the macrocosm, and through the outstretched hands too. And so the cross is the sign for the human being.

And when you find distinguishing marks of the Assyrian kings or of the Egyptian kings, medallions, for instance, then they are medallions with the cross sign.

And similarly with two other signs (the cross on the medallion is one sign that ancient kings wore):

The star in the sign is generally made in such a way that one does not immediately recognize the pentagram in it— or it may even be a hexagram, but that is not the point.

Really clever people have said: that is the sun, that is the cross, that is the moon, that is the star. But the deeper meaning lies precisely in the fact that the human being, the microcosm, is compounded of sun and moon. You see from this ordinary cross, how the concept has been separated from the real object. The direct perception is this, the sign is this: the human being in the form of a cross. People today know so little of how to connect the object with the sign, that, as I have said, an immensely clever literature has come into existence to find out how this sign is connected with what it wants to express. And so one could write fancy articles over the most commonplace words without discovering how these things, these words, are connected with the realities.

Humanity had to go through the period of abstractions. We know that today we are no longer in the sign of Aries, in which the sun stood at the beginning of spring when the transition took place from the old imaginative time, of which echoes still lingered, to the age of abstractions. We have entered the age of Pisces. A special characteristic of this age is that the human being receives the force for abstract ideas out of the macrocosm. Today, this force is given to humanity from the macrocosm. But in the meantime, humans do not know how to reunite the abstract ideas with reality. They *must* be reunited.

I started this lecture by saying that in this fifth post-Atlantean epoch there must be a kind of recapitulation of the time in the Egyptian-Chaldean epoch when people looked back to the ancient Osiris age when Imaginations existed. The reverse, as it were, must take place: humans must find their way back to the Imaginations. Or put differently: Osiris must become alive again, we must find ways

and means to bring Osiris to life. I have spoken very concretely in these studies by saying that we must find forms of
experience which are common to the dead and the living.
Since Osiris was slain he has been with the dead; he will
remain with the dead, but he will have to come again
among the living when concerns arise that are common to
the dead and the living for the social life of human beings.

This brings us to the fact that people must understand
something which is of the utmost necessity for our time to
understand: How will Osiris be revived? How can Osiris
come to new life? How do human beings approach life and
experience again in the imaginative consciousness?

We will speak tomorrow of how Osiris is to rise again,
and how the resurrection is to be brought about. Tomorrow's subject, then, will be the imaginative consciousness.

6 January 1918

IN THESE LECTURES, we have endeavored to understand some aspects of the course of human evolution; we have sought to trace the deeper foundations of such myths as the Osiris-Isis myth; we have further sought to find our way again, from a certain aspect, into the world of the Greek gods. We have touched lightly upon the inner meaning of concepts which perhaps do not come to clear expression, but which underlie the poetic myths of Egypt and Greece, and have sought to study, or at any rate to suggest, the connection between the basis of these myths and the Old Testament doctrines. These Old Testament doctrines have sprung from a different spirit from that of the mythology of the Egyptians and the Greeks. We have seen that the Egyptian and Greek mythologies, in their very structure, are derived from certain ancient experiences of humankind. They are based on a certain consciousness that humanity once possessed—atavistic clairvoyance. Through atavistic clairvoyance human beings had stood in the same inner relation to the spirit pervading nature as later human beings stood, between birth and death, to the objects of sensory perception. We have seen that for this old atavistic knowledge the all-encompassing world conception, which was an inner experience, was more significant than the knowledge based on mere sensory perception of the transitional humanity to which we still belong.

All that had arisen as pictures in the Egyptian and the Greek mythology, better described as visions of the gods, is to be found in the Old Testament as actual doctrine, with morality the keynote. In fact, the day before yesterday, as I spoke of the important difference between the mythology of Egypt and Greece and the Old Testament, I told you that the divine spiritual beings who stand at the beginning of the Old Testament, the Elohim, Yahweh, can only be thought of as together creating humankind. We can only think of them as producing through their deeds what we call earthly humanity. In fact the whole evolution of earthly humanity is accomplished only as a consequence of the fundamental deed of the Elohim, or of Yahweh. I pointed out that this is not the case in Egyptian or Greek mythology. There people looked back into the distant past and said to themselves: The gods Osiris, Isis, Zeus, Apollo, Mars, Pallas, who are now connected with the guidance of human destiny, have arisen from other generations of gods, but human beings were already in existence. The Egyptian and the Greek mythologies traced the human being back to earlier times when those gods recognized in the Egyptians' or the Greeks' own time were not yet creating and ruling. Thus human beings in Egypt and Greece ascribed to themselves an antiquity greater than that of the gods then in power.

This is so fundamental and significant a difference that one must bear it well in mind. In the course of these studies we shall see that this conception points to an infinitely important and significant fact. In the Old Testament doctrine, the gods who were revered were at the same time the gods who created the human race. Only because the Old Testament doctrine makes the Divine the creator of humanity was it possible for the Old Testament doctrine to insert at the same time the moral element, *moral impulse,* into the divine order and hence into the whole ordering of humankind, into Providence, as one would call it now.

This is important for an understanding of the current world conception. For the world concepts of our time are not derived in any very definite way from a uniform source; they have very different origins. We have many belief, which we, as modern human beings, profess to be directly rooted in Greek ideas. We also bear much within us, especially the immediate present bears much in it, that points back to the Old Testament. The human quest, the quest of many human beings, must first involve finding one's way among these often contradictory concepts and ideas, and proceeding through the impulse started by the Mystery of Golgotha. This all lies ahead of us still, and we will have to flesh it out in the time left to us to be together.

It is especially important that we lay one thing as a foundation; I have already referred to it yesterday. We have often mentioned that we are living, since the fifteenth century, in the fifth post-Atlantean epoch; and in a certain sense, I said, certain impulses of the third post-Atlantean epoch, the Egypto-Chaldean, must reappear in the fifth; just as in the sixth post-Atlantean epoch certain impulses of the second, the Zarathustra, the Old Persian epoch will light up, and as in the last post-Atlantean epoch, the seventh, certain impulses of the original Indian epoch will light up again. That is a law in the course of human evolution and it points in a significant manner to the essential features of humanity's spiritual task until the new catastrophe that is to come—such as a natural cataclysm.

Now we have seen in part what immense depth of human consciousness in ancient times is expressed in the fact that these ancient ages evolved the Osiris myth. We have seen that this early age meant to say: a perception once lived among humans through which they could still

directly experience the spiritual in their natural surroundings by way of atavistic Imaginations. That was the age in
which Osiris ruled. But the new perceptions—the Typhon
perceptions, those perceptions that have evolved alphabetical writing from picture writing, those perceptions that
have formed the individually sounding languages from the
primeval sacred language which humans used to speak in
common—have killed what lived in humanity as the Osiris
impulse. So ever since then, Osiris is a being that stands
beside human beings only when they are between death
and a new birth.

We followed the Osiris-Isis legend in its essentials, saw
how Osiris was regarded as a primeval ruler of Egypt who
brought to the Egyptians the most important of their arts,
who ruled in Egypt through long ages, who also travelled
from Egypt into other lands and brought them, not by the
sword but by persuasion, the benefits of the arts taught in
Egypt. While Osiris was away traveling, his wicked brother
Typhon introduced innovations into his own land of Egypt.
And despite the watchfulness of his consort, Isis, when
Osiris returned he was slain by Typhon. Then Isis sought
everywhere for Osiris. Some young boys—the legend
says—told her that the coffin had been carried away by the
sea; she discovered it in Byblos in Phoenicia and brought it
back to Egypt. Typhon had cut up the corpse into fourteen
pieces. Isis collected the pieces; with the use of spices and
by other means she was able to give each piece the appearance of Osiris again. She then induced the priests to accept
a third of the land from her; in exchange for this, they
should keep the grave of Osiris secret and institute the cult
of Osiris, that is to say, a memorial service of the ancient
Osiris time to keep in memory that a different perception
had once existed in humanity. This remembrance was
henceforward to be preserved, and all sorts of secrets sur-
rounded it. The time in which Typhon had slain Osiris was

indicated as the time in November when the sun sets in the seventeenth degree of Scorpio, and opposed to it in Taurus the full moon appears in the Pleiades.

It is further related that Osiris once more betook himself from the Underworld, where he rules over the dead and judges them, to the Upperworld in order to instruct his son Horus, whom he had engendered by Isis. Then Isis let herself be induced to free Typhon, whom she had held imprisoned. Horus, instructed by Osiris, grew so angry at this that he quarreled with Isis his mother and seized the crown from her. Then it is related that either he himself or, in other versions, Hermes, set cow horns upon her head in place of the crown, and since then she has been portrayed with these.

Now, in ancient Egyptian myths you see Isis standing at Osiris's side. And the way the old Egyptians felt about her, she was not only a mysterious deity, a mysterious spirit being who stood in inner relation with the ordering of the world, but she could be said to be the epitome of all the deepest thoughts the Egyptians were able to form about the archetypal forces working in nature and in the human being. When the Egyptians looked up to the great mysteries in their surroundings, they looked up to Isis, whose statue in the temple at Sais has become famous. Beneath this statue stood the well-known inscription meant to express the being of Isis: "I am the All, I am the Past, the Present, and the Future; no mortal has yet lifted my veil."

That was a central thought, especially in the later period of Egyptian civilization. And gazing at the mysteries of Isis, one remembered the other mysteries of the ancient Osiris age. Pious Egyptians trembled at the sight of Isis when they let the words work upon them: "I am the All, I am the Past, the Present, and the Future; no mortal has yet lifted my veil." And when these words worked upon them, the Egyptians remembered at the same time that Isis had once been united with Osiris, when Osiris still wandered upon earth. The uninformed looked upon this as a legend. But in the mysteries, the priests explained that the ancient Osiris time was a time in which the old clairvoyance united human beings with the spirit of nature all about them.

THE LEGEND OF THE NEW ISIS

To understand the Osiris-Isis myth in the present day, we must view it with the sensations and feelings that were in the soul, in the heart, of the Egyptian. We have done so by selecting a few characteristic features. And these characteristic features should bring before our soul's gaze the resonances which once sounded over from ancient times into newer times. While their meaning was lost through the Mystery of Golgotha, they must be clarified again today—precisely for the better understanding of the Mystery of Golgotha. Before our soul's gaze must stand all the mystery that at first could be divined only when the Egyptian felt the words that described Isis: "I am the All, I am the Past, the Present, and the Future; no mortal has yet lifted my veil." We will now contrast this Osiris-Isis myth with another Osiris-Isis myth, quite another one. And in the relation of this other Osiris-Isis myth I must count upon your freedom from prejudice, your impartiality in the highest degree, in order that you not misunderstand it. This other Osiris-Isis myth is in no way born out of foolish arrogance; it is born in humility. It is also of such a nature that perhaps it can only be related today in a most imperfect way. But I will try to characterize its features in a few words.

First of all, it is up to each person—though that can only be provisionally—to decide when to relate this Osiris-Isis myth. I can relate it today only approximately, superficially, even banally. But, as I said, I will try to relate it, disregarding as much as possible any prejudices and calling upon your unbiased understanding. This other Osiris-Isis myth then has somewhat—I say "somewhat"— the following contents.

It was in the age of scientific profundity, in the midst of the land of the Philistines. Upon a hill in spiritual seclusion was erected a Building which was considered to be very remarkable in the land of Philisterium.

(I should just like to say that the future commentator adds a note here that by "the land of Philisterium" not merely the very nearest environment is meant.)

If one wanted to use the language of Goethe, one could say that the Building represented an "open secret." For the Building was closed to none, it was open to all, and in fact everyone could see it at convenient times. By far the greater number of people saw nothing at all. Far the greater number of people saw neither what was built nor what it represented. Far the greater number of people stood before an "open secret," a completely open secret.

A statue was intended to be the central point of the Building. This statue represented a group of beings: the Representative of the Human Being, and a luciferic and an ahrimanic figure. People looked at the statue and, this being the age of scientific profundity in the land of the Philistines, did not know that the statue, in fact, was only the veil for an invisible statue. But the invisible statue itself remained unnoticed by people, for it was the new Isis, the Isis of a new age.

Some few persons of the land of scientific profundity had once heard of this remarkable connection between what was visible and what, in the shape of Isis, was concealed behind the visible thing. And then in their profound allegorical-symbolical manner of speech they asserted that this combination of the Human Figure with Lucifer and Ahriman signified Isis. With this word "signified," however, they not only ruined the artistic intention from which the whole thing was supposed to proceed—for an artistic creation does not merely signify something, but is something—but they completely misunderstood all that underlay it. For the point was not in the least that the figures signified something, but that they already were what they appeared to be. And behind the figures was not an abstraction of the new Isis, but an actual, real new Isis. The figures "signified" nothing at all, but they were in fact, in themselves, that which they made themselves out to be. But they possessed the peculiarity that behind them there was the real being, the new Isis.

Some few who in special circumstances, in special moments, had nevertheless seen this new Isis, found that she was asleep. And so one can say: the real underlying statue concealed behind the external statue is the sleeping new Isis, a sleeping figure—visible, but seen only by a few. Some of them, at very special moments, turned to the inscription, which is in plain view, but which also has been read by only a few people at the spot where the statue stands in readiness. And yet the inscription stands clearly there, just as clearly as the inscription once stood on the veiled form at Sais. And indeed this is what the inscription says: "I am the Human Being, I am the Past, the Present, and the Future. Every mortal should lift my veil."

One day, another figure approached the sleeping figure of the new Isis, and then came back, again and again, somewhat like a visitor. And the sleeping Isis considered this visitor her special benefactor and loved him. And one day she believed in a particular illusion, just as the visitor believed one day in a particular illusion: the new Isis had an offspring, and she considered the visitor whom she looked on as her benefactor to be the father. He regarded himself as the father, but he was not. The visiting spirit, who was none other than the new Typhon, believed that he could acquire a special increase of his power in the world if he took possession of this new Isis. So the new Isis had an offspring, but she did not know its nature, she knew nothing of the being of this new offspring. And she moved it about, she dragged it far off into other lands, because she believed that she must do so. She trailed the new offspring about, and after she had trailed and dragged it through various regions of the world it fell to pieces, into fourteen parts, through the very power of the world.

Thus the new Isis had carried her offspring into the world and the world had dismembered it into fourteen pieces. When the visitor, the new Typhon, became aware of the fact, he gathered together the fourteen pieces, and with all the knowledge of natural scientific profundity, he made a being again, a single whole, out of the fourteen pieces. But this being obeyed only mechanical laws, the law of the machine. Thus a being had arisen with all the appearance of life, but obeying the laws of the machine. And since this being had arisen out of fourteen pieces, it could reproduce itself again, fourteenfold. And Typhon could give a reflection of his own being to each piece, so that each of the fourteen offspring of the new Isis had a countenance that resembled the new Typhon.

And Isis had to follow all this strange affair, half-divining it; half-divining she could see the whole miraculous change that had come over her offspring. She knew that she herself had dragged it about, that she herself had brought all this to pass. But there came a day when she could receive it again in its true, its genuine form from a group of spirits who were elemental spirits of nature; she could receive it back from nature elementals.

As she received her true offspring, which had been stamped into the offspring of Typhon only through an illusion, a remarkable, clairvoyant vision dawned upon her: she suddenly noticed that she was still wearing the cow's horns of ancient Egypt, in spite of having become a new Isis.

And lo and behold, when she had thus become clairvoyant, the power of her clairvoyance summoned—some say, Typhon himself, some say, Mercury. And through the power of the clairvoyance of the new Isis he was obliged to set a crown on her head in the place where once the old crown, which Horus had seized from her, had been, that is to say, on the spot where she developed the cow horns. But this crown was merely of paper—covered with all sorts of writings of a profound scientific nature, still it was of paper. And she now had two crowns on her head, the cow horns and the paper crown embellished with all the wisdom of scientific profundity.

Through the strength of her clairvoyance one day the deep meaning arose in her, as far as the age could reach, of that which is described in St. John's Gospel as the Logos. The Johannine significance of the Mystery of Golgotha arose in her. Through the power of the mystery, the power of the cow horns took hold of the paper crown and changed it into the actual gold crown of genuine wisdom.

These then are the main features that can be given of the new Osiris-Isis legend. I will not of course make myself the commentator who explains this legend. It is the other Osiris-Isis legend. But it must set one thing definitely before our souls. Even though the power of action which is bound up with the new Isis statue is at first weak, exploring and tentative, it is to be the starting point of something that is deeply justified in the impulses of the modern age, deeply justified in what this age is meant to become and must become.

In recent days, we have spoken of the Word's with-
drawal, as it were, from the direct soul experience from
which it originally gushed forth as from a spring. We have
seen how we live in the age of abstractions, when human
words and concepts have only an abstract meaning, when
human beings stand far away from reality. The power of
the Word, the power of the Logos, however, must be recap-
tured. The cow's horns of the ancient Isis must take on
quite a different form.

It is difficult to speak of these things using modern
abstract words. It is better for these things if you try to
bring them before the eye of your soul in such Imaginations as have been brought before you, and to work over
these Imaginations (allowing them to remain Imaginations). It is very important for the new Isis to transform the
cow horns through the power of the Word which is to be
regained through spiritual science, so that even the paper
crown covered with writing in the new, deeply profound
scientific vein, will become a genuine golden crown.

"Now, one day someone came before the provisional
form of the new Isis statue, and up above on the left a
humorous figure had been placed whose mood was a cross
between seriousness, a serious idea of the world, and, yes,
what seemed like a chuckle about the world. And lo and
behold, this person was standing in front of the figure at a
particularly opportune moment, and the figure became
alive and said quite facetiously: Humanity has forgotten it,
but centuries ago already something was proffered to the
new humanity, something about the nature of the new
humanity, insofar as this new humanity still masters only
the abstract word, the abstract concept, the abstract idea
and is far removed from the reality. This new humanity is
limited by words, and is always asking, Is it a pumpkin or is
it a flask?—when it just so happens that a flask has been
made from a pumpkin. The new humanity always clings to

definitions, always stops short at words! In the fifteenth, sixteenth, seventeenth centuries—said the chuckling being—humanity still had some self-knowledge about this peculiar propensity for taking words in a false sense, not relating them to their true reality, but taking them in their most superficial sense. Today, however, humans have forgotten what in those centuries had been put at their disposal in the service of their self-knowledge.

Still chuckling, the being then said: "What modern humanity should take as the true remedy for its abstract spirit is depicted on a tombstone in Moelln in the Lauenburg district. On this tombstone is drawn an owl (*Eule*) holding a mirror (*Spiegel*). And people say that Till Eulenspiegel, after he had wandered performing all sorts of buffoonery and pranks, was buried there. It is said that this Till Eulenspiegel really existed, that he was born in the year 1300, went to Poland, even reached Rome. In Rome he had a wager with the court jesters over all sorts of odds and ends of wisdom and committed all the other Till Eulenspiegelisms, which indeed can be read in the literature about Till Eulenspiegel himself."

Scholars—and scholars are indeed very learned today and take everything with extraordinary gravity and significance—have naturally discovered... oh! they have discovered various things, for example, that Homer didn't really exist. The scholars have naturally also discovered that there never was a Till Eulenspiegel. One of the chief reasons why the actual bones of the actual Till Eulenspiegel (who supposedly was merely the representative of his age) are not supposed to lie beneath the tombstone in Lauenburg on which is depicted the owl with the looking glass, was that another tombstone had been found in Belgium upon which there was likewise an owl with a mirror. Now these learned ones naturally have said, for it is logical, isn't it? (and if they are anything it is logical)—how does it go again in Shakespeare?: For they are all honorable men, all, all, all! Logical they all are!—anyway, so they said: If the same sign is found in Lauenburg and in Belgium, then naturally Eulenspiegel never existed at all.

Generally in life if one finds a second time what one has found a first time, one takes this as a reinforcement. But it is logical, is it not, in these things to take matters so. Well, we say, if I have one franc, then I have one franc. I believe it. So long as I know that I have only a franc, I believe it. But then I get another and I now have two. Now I believe that I don't have any at all! That is the same logic. This in fact is the logic that is to be found in our science... if I were to recount to you where you find this logic, and how very frequently! But what is the essential point of Eulenspiegel's buffoonery? You can look it up in the book: the main thing in Till Eulenspiegel's buffoonery always consists in the fact that Eulenspiegel is given some sort of commission, and that he performs it purely literally and naturally carries it out in the wrong way. For obviously if, for instance, to exaggerate somewhat, one were to say to Eulenspiegel (whom I now take as a representative figure), "Bring me a doctor," he would take the word literally and would bring a person who had graduated as doctor from a university. But he might quite possibly bring a person who was, excuse the strong language, a total idiot, going only by the sound of the word. All the fooleries of Till Eulenspiegel are like this; he only goes by the word taken literally. But this makes Till Eulenspiegel the perfect representative of the present age. Eulenspiegelism is a keynote of our modern times. Words today are far removed from their original source, ideas are often still farther removed, and people do not notice it, but behave in an Eulenspiegel way to what civilization happens to serve up. Which is what made it possible for Fritz Mauthner, in a philosophical dictionary, to argue that all philosophical concepts are

actually merely words, that they no longer have any connection with any kind of reality. People nowadays have no
notion how far what they call ideas, and even "ideals," are
removed from reality. In other words, humanity doesn't
know at all that it has made Eulenspiegel into its patron
saint, that Eulenspiegel is still wandering through the
lands.

One of the fundamental evils of our time rests in the
fact that modern humanity flees from Pallas Athene, that
is, from the goddess of Wisdom, and clings to her symbol,
the *owl* (*Eule*). And humanity no longer has the least idea
of it, but it is true, as I have often shown, that the foundation of external knowledge is merely a reflection—but in a
mirror, it is ourselves that we see!

And so the owl. I mean that the modern scientific profundity, looking into the mirror, into the maya of the
world, sees simply its own owlish face.

These are the things the being at the left above the
modern Isis statue chuckles and snickers over, and many
other matters which, out of a certain human courtesy, shall
not be mentioned at the moment. But I hope to call forth
a feeling that this peculiar representation of human mysteries through the real presence of the luciferic and the
ahrimanic spirits, together with the Representative of
Humanity itself, will arouse a state of consciousness among
humans which wakes those very impulses in the soul that
are necessary for the coming age.

"In the primordial Beginning was the Word, and the
Word was with God, and the Word was a God." But the
word has become phrase, it has withdrawn from its origin.
The word sounds and resounds, but its connection with
reality is not sought; people don't endeavor to investigate
the primary forces of what goes on around them. And one
can investigate these fundamental forces, in the sense of
the present age, only if one realizes that the essences which

we call luciferic and ahrimanic are really bound up with the microcosmic forces of humanity. And one can understand reality today for the human being living between birth and death only if one can form a few ideas of the other reality, which indeed we have often studied, that lies between death and a new birth. For one reality is only the pole of the other reality, the inverted pole of the other reality.

We have mentioned how, in ancient times, when human beings reached maturity, they not only experienced a change such as still occurs today in the change of voice or some other part of the bodily organism, but also underwent an alteration of the soul. We have indicated how the ancient Osiris-Isis myth was in fact connected with the disappearance of this alteration of the soul. What used to arise in humanity through those essences and forces of which we spoke yesterday must come again differently, inasmuch as human beings experience the force of the word, the force of the thought, the force of the idea in a new form. It must not now be something that arises through the forces of nature from the depths of the bodily organization, like the change of voice in the boy, something that embellishes the human being with the power of the animal organization and functions invisibly upon the head as cow horns. No, there must be a conscious grasping by people of the meaning of the Mystery of Golgotha, of the true power of the Word. A new element must be drawn into the human consciousness, radically different from the elements which people still enjoy describing today. This new element, however, will be relevant to the social life, to the pedagogy of humanity, when pedagogy, or the theory of education, comes out of the tragic state in which it exists today.

What does the deeply profound Eulenspiegelism—I should say "natural, scientific profundity"—speak of principally when it speaks of the human being? Of what does even a great part of modern poetry speak? It speaks of the physical origin of the human being in connection with physical beings in the line of descent. Fundamentally the so-called modern, the much-renowned modern theory of evolution is nothing but a conception placing the doctrine of physical descent in the center. For the idea of heredity plays far the greatest role in the theory of evolution. It is a one-sided idea. People are thoroughly satisfied with such one-sidedness, for people think nowadays that in this way one can be very learned. So one can indeed, with quite arbitrary explanations of things, drawn apparently from deep logic, but in reality from misty allusions to the real thing.

Yesterday we saw an example of whole literatures being written because people have lost the connection of a concept with the original experience from which the concept proceeded: the symbol of the cross. A whole literature has been written about it, the cross has been related to everything imaginable. We saw yesterday what it really is about. The same has been done in regard to many other things, and people think themselves very profound when they do it.

I will remind you of one case. Just think how infinitely important many people think themselves to be these days when they believe that they are speaking as we have spoken here today! A fair number of people say, in fact very frequently (you can read it any moment in the papers) and always with great solemnity— "The letter kills, but the spirit gives life." And with this, one thinks one has said something most profound. But one should inquire about the origin of such a saying. It goes back to those times when one had living concepts which indeed still had a connection with what had been undergone and experienced. When one talks today there is little connection, especially between the word and its place of origin. If you want to have a right connection between words and sentences and their origins, then I advise you to read the little book in which "Swiss-German proverbs" have now been collected. One still finds in these popular proverbs an original harmonizing of what is said with the direct experience. By the letter is meant, as you know, the alphabetical script in contradistinction to the ancient kind which the imaginative life drew out of the spirit, as we described yesterday. This ancient spirit gave life, and the liveliness of that epoch of human evolution produced imaginative atavistic clairvoyance. But there was a consciousness that this epoch must in turn be succeeded by another, that the letter must come which would kill the ancient liveliness.

And now relate that with all that I have said about the actual nature of consciousness in connection with death. For the letter kills, but it also brings the consciousness which must be overcome again through another consciousness. The sort of disdainful rejection that modern journalistic folly attaches to the proverb "the letter kills but the spirit gives life" is not what is meant; instead, the sentence is connected with impulses of human evolution. It implies approximately: In ancient times, imaginative times, Osiris times, the spirit kept the human soul in a state of dulled liveliness; in later times the letter called forth consciousness. That is the interpretation of the sentence, that is what it originally meant. And in many instances, just as in this one, people today are very ready with opinions, with arbitrary explanations, because they do not connect anything with them.

This does not prove that what the modern profound scientific method has to say about the idea of heredity is false, only that the other pole must be added when one speaks of heredity. If people point to their childhood, and back from childhood to birth, if they ask themselves, "What do I carry within me?", then the answer is: what parents and ancestors have carried within them and transmitted to me!

There is, however, another way of looking at the human being which we do not as yet practice, which people in the future must practice, and which must be put in the center of pedagogy, the art of education. This is not the looking back at having been younger, but the right consideration of the fact that with every day in life one becomes older. As a matter of fact modern humanity understands only that one has been young once. It does not understand how to grasp realistically that one gets older with every day. For humans do not know the word that must be added to the word heredity when one sets the becoming older opposite the having been young. If one looks to one's childhood, one speaks of what one has inherited; in the same way, when one looks toward the getting older one can speak of the other pole. Just as one speaks of the gate of birth, so one can speak of the gate of death. The one question arises: What have we gained from our forefathers by entering this life through the gate of birth? The other question arises: What perhaps do we lose, what becomes different in us through the fact that we are approaching the coming times, that we get older with every day? What is it like when we consciously experience becoming older with every day?

That, however, is the demand placed on our age. Humanity must learn to become older consciously with every day. For if humans learn to become older consciously with every day, then this really means a meeting with spiritual beings, just as being born and possessing inherited qualities means a descent from physical beings.

I will speak next of the way these things are connected: of that important inner impulse which must draw near the human soul if the soul is to find what is so necessary for the future, what alone can round out and complete the one-sided teachings of natural science.

Then you will see why the new Isis myth can stand beside the old Osiris-Isis myth, why both together are necessary for the humanity of today, why other words must be combined with the words which resound from the statue of Isis at Sais in ancient Egypt: "I am the All; I am the Past, the Present, the Future; no mortal has lifted my veil." Other words must sound into these; they may no longer echo one-sidedly into the human soul today, but in addition must resound the words: "I am Human, I am the Past, the Present, and the Future. Every mortal should lift my veil."

Today I have set before you more riddles than solutions. We will, however, speak of them further and the riddles will then be solved in manifold ways.

8 January 1918

WE SHALL TRY to go somewhat deeper into the matters related to the question that has just been raised: Which particular impulses of human life need to become part of human consciousness in our time as a counterweight to the principle of heredity that has come to dominate almost exclusively in the sciences and also in life more gene-rally? It is a crucial question, but one that needs to be approached slowly and gradually. Actually, this question has the most profound connection with the contrast which I have placed before your mind's eye. On one hand, we have the old Egyptian inscription about the Egyptian Isis: "I am the All, I am the Past, I am the Present, and the Future; no mortal has lifted my veil." And on the other hand, we have, waiting to be taken into our consciousness, the words which from now on must be complementary to the first: "I am the Human Being. I am the Past, the Present, and the Future. All mortals should lift my veil."

Before proceeding any further, we must realize that at the time when the first saying arose in Egyptian culture, to speak of an "immortal" was still clearly to speak of the human being. But in the Egyptian culture, the mystery as a principle of the Mysteries was a deeply rooted principle. The Egyptians who were acquainted with their culture knew that the "immortal" living in the soul must be awakened. But, unlike now, the Egyptians as well as the Greeks—at least the Greeks who shared Plato's thinking—really considered as partaking of immortality only that person who had consciously grasped the spiritual world. You can find evidence for this in my *Christianity as Mystical Fact*, where I quote Plato's occasionally harsh words about the difference between people who try to hold in their soul the impulse of immortality, the spiritual impulse, and those people who disdain or neglect it. Thinking it over, you will easily perceive that the saying on the statue of Sais actually meant that "the person who never seeks to grasp the spiritual element in the soul cannot lift the veil of Isis; but those who grasp spiritual life can lift it, that is, (in the Egyptian sense, for it sounds somewhat different today), those who, being "mortal," make themselves "immortal." There was no intention of saying that the human being as such cannot lift the veil of Isis, but only that one who is exclusively bound to the mortal element, one who will not seek the immortal element, cannot lift the veil. Later on, when Egyptian culture fell into decadence, the saying acquired a mistaken interpretation. As the priests transformed the mystery principle into a power principle, they actually sought to instill into the laity—not the priesthood—the idea that they, the priests, were the "immortals," and those who were not priests were "mortal." In other words, all those standing outside the priesthood were unworthy of lifting the veil of Isis. It is as if in the age of decadence of Egyptian culture, the interpretation had become: "I am the All; I am the Past, the Present, the Future; only a priest can lift my veil." In fact, the priests called themselves the "immortals" in that decadent age.

The use of this expression was abandoned since it applies to human beings living in the physical plane; only the French Academy still uses it, following the Egyptian principle of making especially important persons "immortal." (One is reminded of it at this time because Bergson, who plagiarized Schelling and Schopenhauer, is about to be elevated to the rank of immortal by the French Academy. This is a remnant from an age when these things were still understood running into a time when the words, the concepts, and the ideas have moved very far away from their source.)

Many things will need to be said in the course of these observations, and it might easily look as if my main purpose were to be critical of our times. I have often emphasized that this is not the case. I am characterizing the times, not denigrating them. Still, if we are to speak the truth, one cannot expect that no mention should be made of things that simply must be seen through, whether for their emptiness or for their harmfulness. In fact, we may well ask: Is it really that bad to follow a certain example, albeit from afar, that cannot be followed sufficiently? Does it say in the Gospel that Jesus Christ went into the Temple and flattered the merchants? What we are told is something else—that he overthrew their tables and so on! In order to promote that which must really be promoted, we need to be true to the facts, and point out those things that need to be censured if the age is to progress. We cannot allow ourselves the sentimentality of painting everything in glowing colors, and we certainly should not praise it on the rooftops under the name of universal love.

If we look at things rightly, we can say that on one hand, it just is the case that we live in the materialistic age, and that materialism necessarily leads to abstraction as we have come to know it: that is, the alienation from reality and all the catastrophic consequences in our time of this alienation from reality. On the other hand, it can also be said that of the various periods in the post-Atlantean time, to talk only of these, our fifth period is in some respect the greatest age, one that brings the most to humanity, one that harbors within it immense possibilities for the evolution and existence of humanity. And it is precisely through the things which human beings develop as the shadow side of spiritual life, precisely through those, that human beings make their way into the spiritual world if they proceed rightly. This will, in fact, be the path to the most authentic, the highest of human goals. Evolutionary possibilities in our time are great, greater in some ways than they were in former phases of post-Atlantean evolution. In point of fact, something of immense significance occurred with the beginning of this fifth post-Atlantean period. If we are to give the right coloring to and feel the right nuance of feeling in some of the things we have repeatedly brought up from various viewpoints, we must look in a completely new way at the relationship between the human being and the universe. Of course, the clever ones in Philisterium will call it superstition to speak of a connection between the human being and actual constellations in the cosmos. What matters is to understand that connection rightly. Superstition—what is superstition? The belief that human beings must in some way take their bearings from the universe? We go by the clock, which we regulate from the position of the sun; every time we look at a clock, we practice astrology. There are subconscious members of human nature that take their direction from constellations other than those we go by when in physical life we set our clocks by them. If things are understood rightly, it makes no sense at all to talk of superstition. By way of illustration, I shall now set before your soul a portion of this world-clock. This we will use as a further means of studying the riddle that was first propounded.

The first post-Atlantean cultural epoch arose after the flooding of Atlantis, when the flood, which separates our culture from the Atlantean culture, had receded. The macrocosmic influence on that period was such that the force flowing through earthly life was the one corresponding to the rising of the sun at the vernal equinox in the sign of Cancer. Thus we can say that when the sun entered the sign of Cancer at the vernal equinox, the first post-Atlantean civilization began. It could actually be called "the Cancer civilization," as long as we do not misunderstand the expression. In other words, when the sun rose in the spring, it stood in the sign of Cancer.

We have said earlier that something in the human being always corresponds to things out in the macrocosm. In the human being, Cancer corresponds to the thorax. Speaking in terms of the macrocosm, the first Indian culture was characterized by the fact that it set upon its course while the vernal equinox of the sun was in Cancer. If one were to characterize it from the perspective of the microcosm, one could say that the Indian culture set upon its course at a time when human beings' knowledge of the world, their perceptions, their world view were under the influence of those forces which in the Crab are expressed within the shell of its chest, within its cuirass. Physical human beings today cannot enter into a perceptive and sensitive relationship with the world through the forces of their "crab." If human beings develop the forces that are intimately related to the thorax, if through their thorax they sense all that goes on in nature and in human life, then it will be as if they came into direct touch with the outer world, with all that approaches them from the elemental world. The relation between human beings that underlay the original Indian culture was such that if one human being encountered another, each felt the other's nature, as it were, through the sensitivity of the thorax. The other person was felt to be sympathetic, or more or less antipathetic. Just by breathing the air in a person's surroundings, one would learn to know that person. Modern humanity knows nothing of this, and in some ways it is an advantage. Still, we do each breathe differently in the proximity of another person. For when we are in the proximity of others, we breathe the air expired by them. Modern human beings have become very insensitive to this. But in the Cancer phase of the first post-Atlantean culture, this insensitivity did not exist. A human being could be perceived as sympathetic or antipathetic through his or her breath. My own breath would have moved differently depending on whether the person was sympathetic or antipathetic. And my chest would have been sensitive enough to be aware of its movements.

Just think what one actually perceived! One perceived the other, but one perceived the other through something that took place in oneself. People experienced the other person's inwardness through a process that was perceived as one's own inwardness, one's own bodily inwardness. This was the Cancer culture, illustrated by the example of the meeting of two human beings. But that was the way the whole world was perceived. This was the foundation on which the first post-Atlantean culture was built. A person breathed differently when looking at the sun, when looking at the dawn, when looking at spring, when looking at autumn; and from one's breathing, concepts were derived. And just as modern humanity forms its abstract, its straw-like abstract—not even straw, its paper-abstract— concepts of the sun, moon, and stars, of growth and thriving, of everything imaginable, so in the first post-Atlantean culture, the Cancer culture, human beings formed concepts, but their concepts were felt in this direct way, as co-vibrating with one's own Cancer, one's thorax.

One can say, therefore that if this represents the path of the sun, and the Spring-sun stands in Cancer, then this is the time when the human being also is in a Cancer culture.

Cancer

Every constellation of the Zodiac is related to a particular planet and must be regarded as belonging to that planet. (The reasons for this are probably known by most of you, but I will perhaps mention them presently.) Cancer is considered to be particularly connected to the moon. Since the forces of the moon work in a very particular way when its stands in Cancer, one says that the moon has its house, its home in Cancer. Its forces reside there, and there they are particularly developed.

Now, just as in the human being the thorax corresponds to Cancer, so does the sexual sphere correspond to the planetary moon. In fact, one can say that, whereas on the one hand humans were so susceptible, so receptive and sensitive in the first post-Atlantean epoch, on the other hand, all intimate aspects of the world conception at that time which have come to light are concerned precisely with the sexual sphere. At that time this was appropriate, for there was an innocence which disappeared in later, more corrupt ages.

Then the sun entered the sign of Gemini, the Twins, at the vernal equinox. As long as the vernal equinox continued to be in Gemini, we are dealing with the second, Persian, post-Atlantean cultural epoch. In the microcosmic realm, Gemini was expressed in all that concerns human symmetry, in particular the symmetrical relationship between right and left hand. There are of course other aspects of our being symmetrical; for instance, we see things singly, with our two eyes. This cooperation between right and left, shown particularly in the hands and arms, in the macrocosm corresponds to Gemini.

Now that which the human being takes into life through the forces of Gemini, the forces of symmetry, to make into a world view (just as earlier things were taken in through the thorax), is less closely connected with the person's immediate surroundings. The fact of being symmetrical connects the human being more with what lies away from the earth; not the realm of the earth, but that of the heavens, the cosmic realm. Hence, in the second post-Atlantean epoch, the close connection with the immediate elemental surroundings of the earth fades away, and the Zarathustrian culture appears. This culture was turned toward the cosmos and what is to become Gemini nature—on one hand, to the nature of Light, on the other hand to the nature of Darkness, the twinned natures connected with the forces which the human being expresses through bodily symmetry.

Just as the moon has its house in Cancer, so Mercury has its house in Gemini (see diagram p. 87) And just as in the first post-Atlantean epoch, the force of the sexual sphere helped the human being to form an intimate relationship with the surrounding world, so with the second post-Atlantean epoch help came from the sphere of Mercury, which is connected with the lower body. On the one hand, the human being's forces pass away from the earth into the outer universe, but in this, as it were, the human being is helped by something that is still heavily tinged with atavistic forces, that is, all that is connected with the vascular and digestive systems. The human digestive system is not just for the digestion of food, it is at the same time an instrument of knowledge. We have forgotten these things. And real judgment—not the "feel," of which I have spoken earlier, but real discernment, the deeper gift for combination which creates connection with objects—does not come from the head, but from the lower body, and was of service during this second post-Atlantean period.

Then came the third: the age when the sun at the vernal equinox entered Taurus, the Bull. The forces that descend from the universe when the sun stands in Taurus at the spring equinox are connected in the human microcosm with the regions of the larynx, the forces of the larynx. Hence, in this third post-Atlantean epoch the Egypto-Chaldean human beings developed as their special organ of knowledge all that is related to the larynx. The feeling of relationship between the spoken word and the object, the word and the things out in the universe, was especially strong in that time. These days, in the age of abstractions, it is not easy to form much of an idea of the intimate connection humans established with the cosmos as they knew it through their larynx.

In this case, the forces which correspond to Taurus were assisted by Venus, whose house is in Taurus (see diagram p. 87). In the human microcosm this corresponds to forces which lie between the heart and the stomach. So whatever was known in that time as the cosmic word was intimately connected with human beings, since the latter understood it through the forces of Venus residing in their own body.

There followed the Greco-Latin time, the fourth post-Atlantean epoch. The sun entered Aries, the Ram, at the vernal equinox. In the human being, this corresponds to the head region, the region of the brow, the upper head. A time began during which humans mainly sought to grasp the world through understanding, and this relationship to the world led to thoughts. Head knowledge is very different from earlier forms of knowing. However, despite the fact that the head is an almost exact image of the macrocosm, and in fact precisely because in a physical sense it is an exact reproduction of the macrocosm, it is really of very little value for spiritual purposes. Forgive me for saying so but, being of a physical nature, the human head is worth very little. And whenever human beings rely primarily on their head, all they can produce is an intellectual culture.

The Greco-Latin time brought the head culture to a high point and thus gradually brought the human being into a special relation with the universe, evolving gradually into a full-fledged head and thinking culture, which in turn ran its course, and came to an end. So, from the fifteenth century onward, as I pointed out yesterday, people no longer were able to connect thinking with reality. However, this head culture, this Aries culture, was such that the human being internalized the observation of the universe. As regards the physical world, this Aries culture was most welcome. Only in its decadent form has it became materialistic. The human being in this Aries civilization formed a special relationship with the surrounding world precisely through the head. It is particularly difficult today to understand the Greek culture. Roman culture developed a more commonplace, philistine even, version of it, but we do not realize that, for instance, the Greeks' notion of concepts and ideas was different from ours. I have dealt with this in my *Riddles of Philosophy*.

That Mars had its house in Aries was most significant for that age. The forces of Mars, again, are those connected with the human head, so Mars, who imparts aggressiveness, was particularly supportive of all that developed in the way of a relationship to the world through the head. In the fourth post-Atlantean era, from the eighth century B.C. to the fifteenth century A.D., those conditions were developed which could be described as a Mars culture. The configuration of the social structures that spread over the earth during that time was primarily connected to a Mars culture, a warlike culture. Nowadays, wars are outdated. Although they may be more frightening, they are really stragglers. We shall come back to this.

Now, the human head with all its forces, and as a purely physical thinking tool, is an image of the starry heaven. For this reason, in the fourth post-Atlantean time, there was still something macrocosmic in human thoughts; thoughts were not yet bound up with the earth. But think now of the revolution that happened with the fifteenth century when the Aries culture passed over into Pisces. Pisces forces are those forces in the human being that are connected with the feet. There was a transition from head to feet; it was an immense shift. That is why, if you go back into the time before the fourteenth century with some understanding, and read the alchemical and other writings that are so despised today, you see what deep, what vast insights existed then about cosmic mysteries. But the whole of human culture—and human forces, too—made a complete revolution. What humans had formerly received from the heavens, they now received from the earth. The celestial constellations show us how great a shift had taken place in the human being. And this is connected with the beginning of the materialistic age. Thoughts lose their power, thoughts easily turn into empty phrases.

But now consider another remarkable thing. Just as Venus dwells in Taurus and Mars in Aries, so Jupiter's house is in Pisces. And Jupiter is connected with the development of the human brow, the forehead. If the human being can rise to greatness in the fifth post-Atlantean period, it is precisely because, in the full independence of their humanity, human beings have become able to use the forces of their head to refine and encompass that which was brought to them from the opposite side. In other words, Jupiter performs the same service for humans in the fifth post-Atlantean epoch that Mars did in the fourth. In a certain respect one might say that Mars was king of this world in the fourth post-Atlantean epoch. But in the fifth, he is not the rightful king of this world, because nothing can really be attained through Mars forces in the fifth post-Atlantean epoch. On the other hand, the greatness of this epoch must be brought about through the forces of the spiritual life, world knowledge, world conception. Human beings are shut off from the heavenly forces, confined in the materialistic period. But in this fifth post-Atlantean age, humans have the greatest opportunity of making themselves into beings of the spirit. No age has been as favorable to spirituality as this fifth epoch. All that is needed is courage to drive out the money changers of the Temple. This age must find the courage to set reality, the whole reality, and thus spiritual reality, against the abstractions, against things alienated from reality.

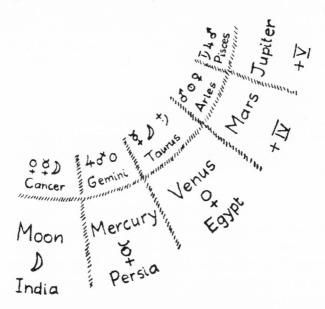

Those who read the stars have always known that particular planets affect various sections of the zodiacal path. There is some justification for assigning to each of these constellations—Moon - Cancer, Mercury - Gemini, Venus - Taurus, Mars - Aries, Jupiter - Pisces—three decanates, as they are called. These three decanates represent those planets which have a particular mission during a particular constellation, while the others remain less active. Thus, for the first post-Atlantean age, the Cancer epoch, Venus, Mercury and the Moon are the decanates; during the Gemini epoch, Jupiter, Mars, the Sun; during the Taurus epoch, Mercury, Moon, Saturn; during the Aries-epoch, Mars, Sun, Venus. During our own epoch, the Pisces epoch, the characteristic decanates, the forces which can serve us the most according to the celestial clock are Saturn, Jupiter, and Mars. Mars, working here differently than when he was in his own house in Aries, is now the representative of human strength. In the outer planets, with Saturn and Jupiter, Mars is connected with the human head, the human countenance, word formation. Thus all that is connected with spirituality for this life between birth and death is especially serviceable in this epoch. This epoch contains the greatest spiritual possibilities. In no other age was it granted to human beings to do as much wrong as in this age, in no other age could one sin more seriously against the inner mission of the time. Anyone living in consonance with the age will use the Jupiter force to transform the forces coming from the earth into a spiritually free humanity. And we have at our disposal the best, the finest powers developed by human beings between birth and death: the Saturn, Jupiter, and Mars forces.

The world clock is favorable to this epoch, but we cannot afford to be fatalistic about things. People cannot say, "Well let's hand ourselves over to world destiny, everything is sure to be all right." Instead, the person who has the will to do so should be prompted to discover endless possibilities in our age. Only, as yet, people have not given much evidence of that will.

But it is just as unfounded to say, "Well, what can I do by myself? The world is just taking its course." And certainly, the world is not paying any attention to us now. But the point I wish to make is a different one. Unlike people thirty-three years (a generation) ago, we cannot say that we won't bother ourselves about anything, for that is the way we came to our current predicament. The point is that each person individually should begin to want to escape from abstraction, to lay aside what is alienated from reality, and to seek—each person alone—to approach reality and get beyond abstraction.

We must move away from farfetched concepts if we are to develop the important matters that will occupy us in the next few days: discussions of the becoming older (aging) of the human being, that is, the going toward death as much as the coming from birth. Today pedagogy, the practical education of children, proceeds entirely from a total concentration on the fact that the child is born and develops as a child; but the time must come when the child learns what it means to become older. It is not at all easy to develop these things. We need to reach further for the necessary concepts. Let us put it this way: to overcome the estrangement from reality which is the signature of our time, it is of the utmost importance for human beings to develop the will to attentiveness, that is , the will to set Jupiter in motion. For that precisely is Jupiter's nature: it is the force that makes a perpetual call on our attentiveness. Human beings are very happy nowadays if they don't need to be attentive, if they can resemble the sleeping Isis—I have mentioned the sleeping Isis deliberately! Most people sleep through the present time and feel very, very comfortable doing so, for they hammer out concepts and then stop short at these, and will no longer pay attention. The important thing to do is to re-examine the relationships that make up life. And the difficult years in which we are living must above all get us away from what weakened human civilization for so long—inattentiveness, lack of will—and make us look at world conditions. It is not sufficient to skim over the surface of things.

For instance, it might easily seem that when I have repeatedly spoken about the harmfulness of Wilsonianism, I was doing so out of some subjective urge. But I am not obeying a subjective urge; it is really necessary today to point the way, away from countless illusionary ideas into the direction where attentiveness must unfold. We are learning from the events of the time; sharpening our attentiveness will allow us to learn from the events of the day an immense amount of what we need in order to understand the great impulses which alone can lead humanity out of the calamities it has brought upon itself. One must ask oneself specific questions, if one wants to pay real attention. The point is not to have some general view of something; what matters is *how* one sees, *how* one can ask questions concerning the external world. Spiritual science has also a practical significance, which gives the impulse to question, to put questions.

These days we read a lot about the so-called peace negotiations in Brest-Litovsk. As you know, all kinds of people participated in them. The chief negotiators from Russia, for example, just to single out a few, are Lenin, Trotsky, a certain Mr. Joffe, and a certain Mr. Kamenev, whose real name is Rosenfeld. Trotsky's name is Bronstein; Joffe is a rich trader from Cherson. It is not unimportant—it is perhaps even important—to consider that Mr. Rosenfeld-Kamenev owes it to pure chance that his head is still upon his shoulders. His head could long since have been sundered from his shoulders. For in November 1914, many delegates were accused in Russia. You could have read about it at the time, and the information has travelled in other ways. Anyway, these delegates were jailed under the accusation of friendship with Lenin, who at the time was abroad, not far from here. At that time, it was believed that

Lenin had declared that "of all evils that can happen to Russia at this time, the fall of Czardom is the least." And so a number of delegates who were known to be corresponding with Lenin were indicted. But it was impossible to arrest them at the time. Of course, all kinds of Russian patriotic words were spoken, words like "Over the heads and mangled bodies of our soldiers, there are traitors who have connection with the shameful Lenin in Switzerland," and so forth. Further proceedings took place in February 1915. Again a number of people were accused, among them a certain Petrovski, also a certain Kamenev, alias Rosenfeld. Kamenev in particular was considered the real Russian traitor type, a particularly abominable fellow. As the proceedings started, there was a general feeling that before long his head would be off his shoulders. But Kamenev-Rosenfeld could prove that, whenever there was talk of war, he had always taken a different stand from Lenin; so too Petrovski. They demonstrated that they had no really serious friendship with Lenin. Kamenev-Rosenfeld in particular was able to prove that he had never wished for a German victory, that only un-Russian crafty comrades like Lenin with foreign interests could desire a German victory, people who felt weak or lazy, but awaited the triumph of freedom from German generals. Those were the words spoken during those proceedings. And a certain Kerenski, who later played another role, was assigned to counsel Petrovski and Kamenev. The charge against both Petrovski and Kamenev-Rosenfeld was high treason, but Kerenski was able to get them off the hook; in his speech we find the following fine words: "The accused were very far from planning to stab in the back those who are ready to die for the Fatherland, they strongly resisted intrigue like the one connected with Lenin's secret confederacy." Kerenski's oratory and other facts that could be brought forward supplied proof that Petrovski and Kamenev had nothing in common with Lenin's views, and they came out of it all with fairly sound skins. Petrovski is now the Minister of the Interior in Lenin's government, and Kamenev, together with Mr. Joffe, is an important negotiator in Brest-Litovsk.

I am quoting these particular stories, and could tell you hundreds and hundreds of similar ones! But the point I wish to make is that it is very important to look at current events. And to get to know current events, we must observe the human beings connected with them—if indeed the things that the men I was just talking about are participating in are really current events. It is very easy to stand back and say, Yes, negotiations are going on in Brest-Litovsk between Russia and the Central Powers. But that is a form of abstraction, it is not the actual event. One approaches the real only when one is willing to pay attention, to look at the concrete detail. I bring this up merely as an example to show that it is also necessary to study present-day history. Everyone these days talks about current events, but how little is really known of the events of the day, how little people actually know of what is going on, how little people even guess at what takes place! It is really astounding, and can be understood only through the unbelievable way in which our intelligence is trained. In fact our intelligence is trained in such a way that in all the sciences people are misled until they form judgements like the one I was describing earlier: If I have one coin, then I have one coin; if I have two coins, then I have none, I have nothing at all! If there is one tomb of Till Eulenspiegel, then he can have lived; if however, there are two tombstones with an owl and a looking glass, it proves that Till Eulenspiegel never lived! If I want to make an electric experiment in the physics classroom, I must carefully dry the machines with warmed cloths so that nothing is damp, for otherwise neither the electrical machine nor the inductive machine would obey me, nor anything else. But then immediately afterwards I say that from out there in the clouds—which are completely drenched and which no professor can have wiped with cloths—lightning comes, and so on. I have often given you examples of the way one person repeats what another has said, without anyone examining it. Thus, for instance, one can hear that the fundamental principle of modern physics is the conservation of energy, of force, and it is traced back to Julius Robert Mayer. These days, physicists and natural scientists and other scholars proclaim him a great hero, but Julius Robert Mayer was once put in a lunatic asylum because he had published "absurd trash," had claimed to have discovered a new principle. He really was incarcerated in a lunatic asylum! The great credit due him went to some university rector, but I will not stress this any further; it often happens, as you well know. What I will stress is this: again and again one sees, "Conservation of energy—Julius Robert Mayer discovered it." No one reads, but each person repeats what has been said. In Mayer's work nothing is stated at all in the precise form in which the energy principle is presented today, but it is there in a very different formulation, in fact a very reasonable formulation.

Another example lies near our subject. Dr. Schmiedel has given me a magazine article which supports Goethe's theory of colors. Two learned gentlemen assert there that Goethe knows nothing of the Fraunhofer lines; yet Dr. Schmiedel has put together four columns consisting entirely of passages from Goethe in which he speaks of the Fraunhofer lines! But the learned gentry talk, they pass judgment on the range of Goethe's optical information, and they drift into such judgments: Goethe did not know of the Fraunhofer lines. They tell people impudent falsehoods, for in this so-called "authority-free" age, what a scientist says is gospel, just as for many people what politicians say is gospel, and for the politicians what Woodrow

Wilson says is gospel. So it is enough these days for someone just to say, Goethe did not know of the Fraunhofer
lines. Nor is it necessary to prove it to people. For very
soon, another person will repeat it, and then another, and
then a fourth. The inattention, the thoughtlessness with
which people live these days is indeed great, while the
willingness to look at the concrete is not forthcoming.
Moreover humanity is much too inclined to take a lively
interest in abstractions, to become enthusiastic through
abstractions.

I have merely introduced here what is yet to occupy us—
the important idea which must enter the culture of our
time and our pedagogy, the principle of human beings
becoming old in their physical bodies, which is linked with
their becoming younger in their etheric bodies. We shall
speak of this in detail next time.

11 January 1918

OUR AIM in these lectures is to speak of important questions of human evolution, and you have already seen that all sorts of preliminary facts drawn from distant sources are necessary for our purpose. In order that we may have as broad a foundation as possible, I shall remind you today of various things that have been said from one or another standpoint during my stay here, but which are essential for a right understanding of the next two lectures.

I have pointed out to you that in the evolutionary course of humanity which can be regarded as primarily interesting us after the great Atlantean catastrophe, significant changes took place in humanity. Some months ago I indicated how changes in humanity as a whole differ from changes in a single individual. As the years go by, the individual becomes older. In a way, one can say that for humanity the reverse is the case. A human being is first a child, then grows up and attains the age known to us as the average age of life. In so doing, the human being's physical forces undergo many changes and transformations. We have already described in what sense a reverse path is to be attributed to humanity. One can say that during the time following the great Atlantean cataclysm—geologists call it the Ice Age, religious traditions the Flood—during the time immediately following the great flooding of the earth, a real mutation took place, so that over the next 2,160 years human beings were capable of developing in very different ways than was to be the case later.

We know that at present, independently of our own actions, we can develop up to a certain age; we are capable of development by dint of our nature, of our physical forces. We have stated that in the first epoch after the great Atlantean cataclysm, humans remained capable of development for a much longer time. They remained so into their fifties, and they always knew that the process of aging was connected with a transformation in their soul and spirit. If today we wish to develop our soul and spirit after our twenties, we must willfully seek this development. We become physically different in our twenties, and in the process of becoming different, something comes to life and determines the progress of our soul and spirit. Then we lose our dependency on the physical; our physical nature, so to speak, stops providing for us, and any further advance must happen through our own willpower. This, at least, is how things look from the outside—we shall see immediately how matters stand inwardly.

Things were quite different in the first 2,160 years after the great Atlantean catastrophe. Human beings were still dependent on the physical element far into old age, but they enjoyed that dependence. They had the joy not only of progressing during their growth, but also of experiencing even in the decline of their life-forces the fruit of these declining life-forces as a kind of blooming of qualities of the soul, which human beings no longer can feel. Then came a time when humans remained capable of development only into their fifties. For the external physical and cosmic conditions of human existence changed in a relatively short time.

In the second epoch after the catastrophe, that is, for another 2,160 years or so, during the Old Persian epoch,

humans remained capable of development until their for-
ties. In the next period, during the Egypto-Chaldean
epoch, humans evolved until the age of thirty-five to forty-
two years. During the Greco-Roman period, the span
reached to approximately thirty-five years. Since the fifteenth century, human beings develop into their twenties.

External history does not tell us anything about this,
nor does historical science believe it, yet an infinity of mysteries of human development are connected with it. One
might say that the whole of humanity is getting younger
and younger. We have seen what the consequences of this
would be. Those consequences were not so pressing in the
Greco-Roman age; a person remained capable of development up to the thirty-fifth year. But they are becoming
more and more pressing, and are especially significant in
our time. Humanity as a whole is living, so to say, in the
twenty-seventh year, pushing twenty-six, and so on. Human
beings are condemned to carry right through life whatever
development of their natural forces has taken place in
early youth, unless, of their own free will, they take their
further development in hand. And the future of humanity
will consist in human development receding further and
further, so that a time will come when the views and opinions of youth will prevail, unless a new spiritual impulse
takes hold of humanity.

We can observe external symptoms in humanity of this
becoming younger. Anyone who looks at historical development with more sharpened senses can observe this process—it is observable in the fact that in ancient Greece, for
instance, a man still had to have reached a certain age
before he could take part in public affairs. Today, large seg-
ments of humanity are demanding that this age be lowered
as much as possible, since it is felt that people in their
twenties already know everything there is to know. These
demands will keep increasing, and unless some insight

arises to slow them down, we will hear the claim not only that people in their twenties are clever enough to participate in parliamentary business, but that even eighteen- and nineteen-year-olds contain in themselves all that a human being can encompass.

At the same time, this kind of growing younger challenges human beings to draw to themselves from the spirit what is no longer given by physical nature. Last time, I called your attention to the momentous break in the evolutionary history of humanity represented by the fifteenth century. Again, here is something of which external history gives no tiding, for external history, as I have often said, is a *fable convenue*. There must be an entirely new knowledge of the being of humanity. For only when such a new knowledge is attained will humanity find the impulse it needs if it is to take in hand of its own free will what nature no longer provides. We cannot allow ourselves to believe that the future of humanity will come from the thoughts and ideas which the modern age has brought, and of which it is so proud. One cannot do enough to become fully aware of the necessity to seek for fresh and different impulses for the evolution of humanity. It is of course trivial to say, as I have often remarked, that our time is a transition age, for, in reality, each age is an age of transition. But it is a different thing to know precisely what it is that changes in a particular age. Every age is indeed a transitional age, but in each age one should look and see what specifically is passing over.

I will link this to one fact. I could take hundreds of others from every part of Europe, but I will take one specific fact and let it serve as an example. In 1828 in Vienna, a number of lectures were given by Friedrich Schlegel, one of the two Schlegel brothers who served Central European culture so well. In these lectures, Schlegel sought to show from a lofty historical standpoint what the development of the time required, and how these requirements should be given attention if the right direction were to be given to the evolution of the nineteenth century and the coming age.

At the time, Friedrich Schlegel was influenced by two main historical impressions. On the one hand, he looked back at the eighteenth century, how it gradually evolved to atheism, materialism, irreligion. He saw how what had gone on in people's minds during the course of the eighteenth century ultimately exploded in the French Revolution. This, by the way, is not meant as a criticism of Schlegel, but merely as a factual description, a nonjudgmental description of a human outlook. Schlegel saw a great one-sidedness in the French Revolution. To be sure, we might find it reactionary for a man like Schlegel to see the French Revolution as a great one-sidedness, but we would also have to look at such a verdict from other aspects. On the whole, it is fairly simple to tell oneself that this or that or the other was gained for humanity by the French Revolution. It is no doubt very simple; but there is a question whether someone who speaks thus enthusiastically about the French Revolution is altogether sincere in his inmost heart. A crucial test of this sincerity is this: one should consider how one would look at such a movement if it broke out around one in the present day. What would one say then? One should really ask this question of oneself when judging these matters. Only then does one have an acid test of one's own sincerity, for on the whole it is really not very difficult to be enthusiastic about something that went on so many decades ago! The question is whether one would be equally enthusiastic if one had to partake of it now.

As I said, Friedrich Schlegel looked upon the French Revolution as the explosion of the so-called Enlightenment, the atheistic Enlightenment of the eighteenth century. Side by side with this event, he set another: the appearance of the man who replaced the Revolution, and who contributed so enormously to the later shaping of Europe—Napoleon. From the lofty standpoint from which he viewed world history, Friedrich Schlegel pointed out that when such a personality enters with such force into world evolution he must be considered from a different viewpoint than the one generally taken. He makes a very fine observation when speaking of Napoleon: "One should not forget that Napoleon had seven years in which to grow familiar with what he later looked on as his task; for twice seven years the tumult lasted that he carried through Europe, and then, he was granted seven more years after his fall. Four times seven years, thus was the career of this man."

I have indicated on various occasions the role of this inner law in the case of persons who are really representative in the historical evolution of humanity. I have pointed out to you how remarkable it is that Raphael always makes an important painting after a definite number of years. I have pointed out that Goethe's poetic powers always flare up in seven-year periods, whereas between these times there is a dying back. One could bring forth many such examples. And note that Schlegel did not look on Napoleon exactly as an impulse of blessing for European humanity.

Now in his lectures, Friedrich Schlegel shows what Europe needs to recover from the confusion brought by the Revolution and the Napoleonic Age. And he finds that the deeper reason for the disorder lies in the fact that human beings cannot lift themselves to a more all-embracing standpoint in their world conception, which indeed could come only from a deeper understanding of the spiritual world. The way Friedrich Schlegel sees it, the consequence was that instead of a shared human world conception, we have everywhere party platforms in which everyone looks on his or her point of view as an absolute, something which is bound to bring salvation to all. According to Friedrich Schlegel, the only salvation for humankind would be for each human being to be aware that he or she takes a certain standpoint and others take others, and any agreement has be the outgrowth of life itself. No single point of view should gain a footing as an absolute.

Now according to Friedrich Schlegel, true Christianity is the one and only thing that can show people how to realize the tolerance he has in mind—a tolerance inclining not to indifference, but to strong and active life. And therefore he draws the following conclusion, and I must always emphasize that this is in 1828: the whole life of Europe, but especially the life of science and the life of the State must be Christianized. He sees the great evil in the fact that science has become un-Christian, that states have become un-Christian, and that nowhere has the true Christian impulse permeated scientific thinking or the life of the State. And he demands that the Christ Impulse should once again permeate scientific life and the life of the State.

Friedrich Schlegel was of course speaking of the science of his time and of the State of his time, 1828. But for reasons which will be clearer to us very soon, one could look at modern science and modern political life as he regarded them in 1828. Try for once to inquire whether the sciences that count the most in public life—physics, chemistry, biology, economy, political science—take the Christian impulse seriously anywhere within them! People do not acknowledge it, but all the sciences are actually atheistic. And the various churches tag along with them, as they do not feel strong enough to really permeate science with the principle of Christianity! Hence the cheap and comfortable theory that the religious life makes demands different from those of science, that science must keep to the observable, religion to the feelings. Both are to be nicely separated, one direction is to have no say over the other. This way, we can all live together—we can indeed, but it gives rise to the sort of conditions that exist now!

Now Friedrich Schlegel's contribution at that time was imbued with deep inner warmth, imbued with his great personal impulse to serve his age, to help things along, to ensure that religion would not just be a Sunday school, but would be brought into all of life, and particularly into science and into political life. And from the way Schlegel spoke then in Vienna, one can see that he felt hopeful that from the confusion started by the Revolution and Napoleon a Europe would arise whose scientific and political life would be Christianized. The final lecture treated especially the prevailing spirit of the age and the forthcoming general revival. And as the motto for the lecture, which was powerfully delivered, he put the Biblical quote, "I come quickly and I make all things new." And he used this motto because he believed that in the young people of the nineteenth century, whom he was addressing, lay the power to receive that which can make all things new.

Anyone who reads through Friedrich Schlegel's lecture, leaves them with mixed feelings. On the one hand, one says: How lofty the standpoints, how lucid the conceptions of the men who formerly spoke of science and political life! How one must have longed for such words to kindle a fire in countless souls. And had they kindled this fire what would Europe have become in the course of the century? But I repeat: one leaves with mixed feelings. For, in the first place that is not what came about; what came about are the catastrophic events that now stand so terribly before us. And these catastrophes were preceded by a preparation in which anyone could have exactly seen that such events had to come. They were preceded by the age of materialistic science, which had become even stronger than it had been in Friedrich Schlegel's time, and by the age of materialistic statesmanship over the whole of Europe. And it is with sorrow that one now beholds the motto "For lo, I come quickly and make all things new."

There must have been a mistake somewhere. Certainly, Friedrich Schlegel spoke from utter conviction. And he was an exceptionally sharp observer of his time. He was able to judge the circumstances—but yet something must not have been quite right. For what did Friedrich Schlegel understand by the Christianizing of Europe? We can admit that he had a feeling for the greatness, the significance of the Christ-Impulse. He also had the feeling that the Christ-Impulse must be understood in a new way in a new age, that we cannot stop short at the way earlier centuries had grasped it. He knew that; he unquestionably had a feel for that. Nevertheless, with this feeling, he leaned back onto Christianity as it already existed, Christianity as it had developed historically in his time. He believed that from the Vatican a movement could start of which it could be said, "I come quickly and make all things anew." He was in fact one of those nineteenth-century men who turned to Catholicism from Protestantism because they believed they could trace more strength in Catholic life than in the Protestant. But he was free spirit enough not to become a Catholic zealot.

There is, however, something which Friedrich Schlegel did not say to himself. What he failed to say to himself was that one of the deepest and most significant truths of Christianity lies in the words "I am with you always even unto the end of the earth's time." Revelation has not ceased; it returns periodically. And whereas Friedrich Schlegel built upon what was already there, he should have seen, he should have felt that a real Christianizing of science and of the life of the State could take place only if fresh knowledge was drawn in from the spiritual world. He did not see this; he knew nothing of it. And this example, one of the most

significant examples from the nineteenth century, shows us
that, again and again, even the most enlightened minds fall
prey to the illusion that it is possible to latch onto something already existing. We think that there is no need to
fetch something new out of the fountain of youth. With
these illusions, people can of course say things and carry
out things that are great and brilliant, but it leads nowhere.
Friedrich Schlegel hoped that nineteenth-century Europe's
science and political life would be permeated by Christianity. It must come quickly, he thought, this general renewal
of the world, a general restoration of the Christ-Impulse.
And what happened? A materialistic trend in the science of
the second half of the nineteenth century, which made the
ambient materialism Friedrich Schlegel had known in 1828
seem mere child's play. And a materializing of political life
took place (we must know history, *real history*, not the *fable
convenue* which is taught in schools and universities), of
which likewise he could see nothing around him in 1828.
Thus he prophesied the Christianizing of Europe, and was
such a bad prophet that the materializing of Europe came
about instead!

Human beings willingly live in illusions. And this is
related to the main problem occupying us, the problem
that will become clear in the next few days: human beings
have forgotten how to become truly old, and we must learn
again how to become old. We must learn to become old in
a new way, and can do so only through a spiritual deepening. But, as I said, this will become clearer in the course of
our study. Our time is generally disinclined to it, but it
must grow inclined for it.

In any case the forms of thought and feeling customary
nowadays do not make it easy for people to familiarize
themselves with, for instance, the spiritual challenge of
anthroposophical spiritual science. This can be shown from
various examples; here is one that lies to hand.

The day before yesterday, I received a letter from a man of learning. He writes to me that he has just read a lecture of mine on the task of spiritual science, given two years ago,[1] and that he now sees that this spiritual science has after all something very fruitful for him. The letter has a thoroughly warm tone, a thoroughly kind, amiable tone. One sees that the man is gripped by what he has read in the lecture on the task of spiritual science. He is a trained natural scientist, a man of today, and he has seen from this lecture that spiritual science is not stupid or impractical, but can give an impulse to the time. But now let us look at the reverse side of the matter. Five years ago, the same man had attempted to connect himself with spiritual science, to join a group where spiritual science was being studied, and had begged at that time to have conversations with me, which he had. He took part in meetings five years ago, and his reaction was such that the whole matter became totally repugnant to him, and he turned away so strongly that in the meantime he has become an enthusiastic panegyrist of Herr Freimark, whom you know from his various writings. Now the same man excuses himself by saying that it would perhaps have been better if, instead of doing what he did, he had read some books of mine and made himself acquainted with the subject. But he had not done that, he had judged by what others had told him, and had gotten such a forbidding picture of spiritual science that he found it not at all suited to his own path of development. Now, five years later, he reads a lecture, and finds this not to be the case at all.

I quote this example, and there could be many more, of the way in which people relate to what in our time desires a Christianizing of the sciences, a Christianizing of all

---

1. *The Mission of Spiritual Science and of Its Building at Dornach.* London: H.J. Heywood-Smith, 1917.

political life—not in the sense Friedrich Schlegel meant it, but in the only viable way. I give this as an example of the thought habits of our time, in particular of the scientific thinking of our time. Here is a man who approached the anthroposophical movement, had some talks, took part in group meetings, felt disgruntled about the participants in these meetings and what they had to say to him, concluded that he had to accuse anthroposophy as a whole, and became an enthusiastic panegyrist of Herr Freimark, who has written the vilest articles about spiritual science. Five years later the same person decides to really read something! In other words, the fact that some people today are abusive or agree with the abuse is no proof that deep down they might not have a natural tendency to attach themselves to anthroposophical spiritual science. If they have as much good will as the man in question, it will take them five years; some need ten, some fifteen, many fifty, and many so long that they can no longer experience it in this incarnation. You see how little people's behavior is any kind of proof that they are not seeking what can be found in anthroposophical spiritual science.

I bring up this example because it points to the profoundly important fact I have often mentioned; namely that people do not have an easy time getting to the heart of the matter, that they hold on to inherited prejudices which they will not let go! And that is connected with other matters, too. One need only transpose oneself in feeling into those ancient times of which I spoke earlier today and on the previous days. Think of a young man right after the Atlantean cataclysm in his connection with other people. He was, say, twenty, twenty-five years old; near him was someone forty, fifty or sixty years old. He could say to himself: What a happiness it will be someday to be as old as that, for as one lives one goes on experiencing more and more! There was a perfectly obvious, immense veneration for one who had grown old; a looking-up to the aged, linked with the consciousness that they had something else to say about life than younger people did. It is not enough to understand this theoretically; what matters is to have it in one's own feelings, and to grow up under this impression. It is of infinite consequence to grow up in such a way as not merely to look back at one's youth and say, Ah! how fine it was when I was a child! This beauty of life will never be taken from human beings by any kind of spiritual reflection. But it is a one-sided reflection which, in olden times, was supplemented by the other: How beautiful it is to become old! For to the same degree that one became weaker in body, one grew into strength of soul, one grew into union with the wisdom of the world. At one time this was an accepted part of training and education.

Let us now look at another truth which I have mentioned here and there to our friends, although I have not talked about it this week yet: We grow older, but only our physical body grows older. For from a spiritual standpoint, it is not true that we grow older. It is a maya, an illusion. It is certainly a reality in respect to physical life, but not in respect to the full nature of a human being's life. Yet we have the right to say this only if we know that the human being who lives in the physical world between birth and death is something more than just a physical body. He consists also of higher members than that, which we call the etheric body or body of formative forces, and then the astral body, the ego. Let us stop at these four parts.

But even if we stay with the etheric body, the invisible, supersensitive body of formative forces, we see that we carry it within us from birth to death, just as we carry about our physical body of flesh and blood and bones. We carry in us this etheric body of formative forces, but there is a difference: the physical body grows ever older, the etheric body is old when we are born; in fact, if we examine its true nature, it is old then and becomes younger and younger. So one can say that our primary spiritual members become steadily stronger and younger as the physical-corporeal members become weak and powerless. And it is true, literally true, that when our faces begin to get wrinkled our etheric body blooms and becomes chubby-cheeked.

Of course, the materialist thinker could say that this is completely contradicted by the fact that it is impossible to perceive it! In ancient times, nature itself brought it about in due course; in modern times, it is almost an exception. But even so, there are exceptions. I remember speaking once of a similar subject at the end of the 1880s with Eduard von Hartmann, the philosopher of the "Unconscious." We came to speak of two men who were professors at the Berlin University. One was Zeller, a Swabian then seventy years old, who had just petitioned for his pensioning, having gotten it into his mind that "I got so old I can no longer hold my lectures." At seventy-two, he was indeed old and frail. And the other was Michelet, who was ninety-three years old. And Michelet had just been with von Hartmann and had said, "Well, I don't understand Zeller! When I was as old as Zeller I was just a young fellow, and now, only now do I really feel fitted to say something to people.... As for me, I shall still lecture for many long years!" But Michelet had something in him of what can be called "having grown young in forces." There was of course no inner necessity for him to grow that old; for instance, a tile from a roof might have killed him when he was fifty years old or earlier. But, having grown that old, in his soul he had in fact not grown old, but precisely young. Michelet, however, in his whole being was no materialist. Even Hegel's followers have in many ways become materialists, not that they would agree. But Michelet, although he spoke in difficult sentences, was inwardly gripped by the spirit. Only a few, however, can be so inwardly gripped by the spirit. But this is just what anthroposophical spiritual science is seeking: to give something that can be of value to all human beings, just as religion must be of value to all human beings. But this is connected with our whole training and education.

Our whole educational system is built entirely on materialistic impulses—and this must be seen in a much broader perspective than is generally done. Only people's physical bodies are considered, never their becoming younger in spirit. No account is taken of one's growing younger as one grows older! At first glance, this is not always immediately evident. Nevertheless, all that has been built up into the subject matter of pedagogy and education considers human beings only in their youth, unless they happen to become professors or scientific writers. Rarely does one find people who care to take up in later life, when they no longer need it, the material which is presently absorbed in one's school days. I have known doctors who were leaders in their specialty, that is, they had so passed their student years that they had become leaders in the field. But there was no question at all of their continuing the same methods of acquiring knowledge in later years. I once knew a very famous man—I will not mention his name, he was so renowned—who stood in the front rank of medical science. He made his assistant attend to the later editions of his books because he himself no longer took part in science; that did not suit his later years.

This is connected however with something else. We are gradually developing a consciousness that what one can absorb through learning is really of service only in one's youth and that one gets beyond it later. And this is the case. One can still force oneself to turn back to many things, but then one must really force oneself; as a rule, it doesn't come naturally. And yet, unless a person is always taking in something new—not just getting it through the concert hall, the theater, or, with all due respect, the newspaper or something of that kind—then that person grows old in soul. We must absorb in another way, the soul must really feel that it experiences something new, unformed, and that one can react to what one takes in just as the child reacts. This cannot be done artificially; it can happen only when one can approach something in later life precisely as one approaches ordinary educational subjects as a child.

But now, take anthroposophical spiritual science. We need not puzzle our heads over what it will be like in later centuries; the right form will be found in due time. But in any case, the way things stand now, however many people may dislike it, there is no primary necessity to cease absorbing it. No matter how aged one may have become, one can always find in it something new that grips the soul and makes it young again. And many new things have already been found on spiritual, scientific soil—even things that let one probe the most important problems of the day. But mostly, the present needs an impulse which seizes the person directly. Only in that way can the present time come through the calamity upon which it has entered, with such disastrous effects. The impulses in question must approach human beings in a direct fashion.

And now, if one is not Friedrich Schlegel, but a person with some insight into humanity's true needs, one can nevertheless keep in mind several of Schlegel's beautiful thoughts and rejoice in them. He said that things must not be treated as absolutes from a single standpoint. At first, he saw only the political parties which regard their own principles as the only ones that can guarantee universal happiness. But in our time, many more things are being treated as absolutes! Above all, a perception is lacking that in life an impulse might be harmful on its own, yet be beneficial in cooperation with other impulses, because it then turns into something else. Think, if you will—and I will make a sketch—of three tendencies which run concurrently.

The first direction will symbolize for us the socialism toward which modern humanity is striving, although it is not precisely the current popular, or Leninist, socialism. The second line symbolizes what I have often described as freedom of thought, and the third direction is spiritual science. These three things belong to one another; they must work together in life.

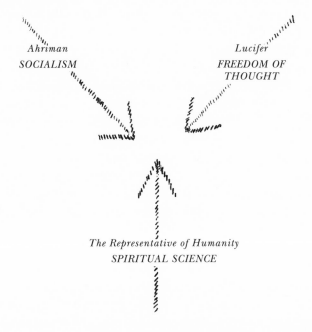

If socialism, in the crude materialistic form in which it appears today, attempts to force itself upon humanity, it would bring down the greatest unhappiness upon humanity. It is symbolized for us by the Ahriman figure in the group sculpture, it represents Ahriman in all his forms. If the false freedom of thought which wants to stop short at every single thought and hold it for valid, seeks to force itself on humanity, then again, harm is brought upon humanity. This is symbolized in our group by Lucifer. But you can exclude neither Ahriman nor Lucifer from the present day, although they must be balanced by pneumatology, by spiritual science, which is symbolized by the Representative of Humanity in the sculpture. I must repeatedly point out that spiritual science is not meant to be merely something for people who have cut themselves adrift from ordinary life through some circumstance or other, or who want to be stimulated a little by exposure to all sorts of things connected with higher matters. Instead, spiritual science, anthroposophical spiritual science is meant to be connected with the deepest needs of our age. For the nature of our age is such that its forces can be discovered only by looking into the spiritual world. This is connected with the worst evil of our time—which is that countless people have not the slightest idea that social, moral, historical life is ruled by supersensible forces; indeed just as there is air all around us, so too supersensible forms hold sway around us. The forces are there, and they demand that we receive them consciously, in order to direct them consciously; otherwise they can be led astray by the ignorant, or those who lack understanding. In any case, the matter cannot be trivialized. We must beware the idea that one can point to these forces the way some people tell the future from reading coffee grounds, and so forth! Nevertheless, in a certain way, and sometimes in a very close way, the future and its shaping are connected with realities which can be known only by starting with the principles of spiritual science.

People will perhaps need more than five years to see this. But it is simply a fact—and I realize this may sound ridiculous to you as I say it, although in any case the day will come when it will be possible to acknowledge it—that what is now heard as Wilson's call to arms had been predestined to happen. And there are people in this room who can attest to the fact that this call to arms was thought about in the right way. It is not easy to talk about those things, but the events of our time keep calling our attention to the fact that people need to note that some things can be understood and judged rightly only from the standpoint of anthroposophical spiritual science.

12 January 1918

THE MATTERS NOW under discussion are connected with a fact that may seem strange at first hearing, but which corresponds to a deep and significant truth—namely, the human being wanders over the earth but has in reality no true understanding of him- or herself. In its unmitigated form, this statement applies particularly to our own time. We know that in Ancient Greece, the great and significant inscription "Know Thyself" stood on Apollo's temple as a challenge to those who sought for spiritual enlightenment. Nor was this "Know Thyself" on the Delphic temple merely a phrase at that time, as we know from our various studies. For even in that age it was still possible to obtain a deeper knowledge of the human being than is possible at the present time. But this present time is a challenge for us to strive again for real knowledge, for a knowledge of the true nature of the human being on earth.

Now, it would seem hard to understand the things which must be said in connection with this issue, but they are not really difficult, despite the fact that they sound forbidding. The problem is that, today, when we speak of understanding it always comes down to our attempting to understand through abstract concepts; something else is required to understand the human being. One must open oneself to taking in the image, as it were, of the human being wandering upon the earth, to taking it in as a picture which expresses something, which discloses something, which wants to reveal something to us. We must revive the consciousness that the human being is a riddle waiting to be solved. We shall not, however, solve the riddle of the human being if we remain as indolent, as theoretical in our thinking as we now like to be. For the human being, as we have stressed again and again, is a complicated being. The human being is more, vastly more, than the physical form that wanders in front of our eyes as human being—the human being is far, far more than that. Nonetheless, this physical structure that walks about in front of our eyes and which we call human, this physical form and all that belongs to it, is an expression for the whole comprehensive human being. Not only is it possible to recognize in the physical form that goes about among us what the human being is between birth and death in the physical world, but, if one only will do so, it is also possible to recognize in the human being the immortal, eternal being of soul. All that is required is that one develop a feeling for the complexity of that human form. Our modern science which is popularized and thus accessible to all is not fitted to call forth a feeling for what a miraculous structure this human being actually is, who wanders on earth. We must regard the human being quite differently.

You have assuredly seen a human skeleton; remember then that the skeleton has two parts, if one disregards everything else. Of course much more can be said about the matter, but, leaving other things aside, the skeleton is a duality. You can easily lift the skull off the skeleton; it is merely set above it, and then you are left with the human being, minus a skull. It is very easy to lift off the skull. The rest of the human being is still a very complex being, but we shall now consider it as a unity and leave aside its complexity. But first, let's look at the duality which we see when we look at a human being as, say, head-human and trunk-human. The complete flesh and blood human being is also a duality.

Now, spiritual scientists need not be so fond of comparisons as to treat them as absolutes and develop them into metaphysical systems—we won't do that, but the use of comparisons is to make some things clearer. So it is perfectly natural, since it corresponds to the testimony of our eyes, to say that in respect to the head, the human being is ruled by the spherical form. If we express in a schematic drawing what the human head is, we can say: the human being is ruled by the spherical form.

A diagram of the rest of the body would naturally have to pay attention to the complications, but we will not do that today. You will however see easily that, disregarding certain complications, just as the human head can be represented by a sphere, so the rest of the human being can be represented by a moon form, only of course the relative position of the two forms will vary with the corpulence of the individual!

In any case, we can conceive of the human being as spherical form, and as moon form. There is deep inner justification for that; however we will not discuss this right away, but only think of the fact that the human being falls into these two members.

Now the human head is first of all a true apparatus for spiritual activity; all that the human being can produce in the way of thoughts and feelings is done through the "machine" of the human head. But we would never be able to understand the substance of the human being by mere reference to the things that the head, as machine, can produce in the way of thoughts, feelings, and so forth. In fact, if we were told to use only the head as the tool of our spiritual life, we would never be in a position to talk about ourselves as "I." For what is the head? In truth, as we encounter its globular form, the head is a representation of the whole cosmos as it appears to you, complete with all its stars, its planets and comets, and even meteorites—for there are irregularities in many heads. The human head is an image of the macrocosm, an image of the whole world. And I have mentioned this in other contexts, although only contemporary prejudice is totally ignorant of the fact that the whole world contributes to the making of a human head.

But if through heredity, through birth, this human head is transported to earth, it cannot be an apparatus for comprehending the human being. We have been given in our head an apparatus which is like an extract of the whole world, but which is not competent to comprehend the human being. Why? Well, because the human being is more than we can see and think with the head. People often say these days, "There are limits to human knowledge, you can't get beyond these limits!" But this is only because they reckon with the wisdom of the head, and the wisdom of the head does not go beyond certain limits. This wisdom of the head has also produced what we described a few days ago as the Greek gods. The Greek gods were the product of the wisdom of the head. They are the gods from above, meaning they are gods only for that part of the human being which the head and its wisdom can encompass.

I have often called your attention to the fact that besides this external mythology the Greeks also had their Mysteries. In the Mysteries, the Greeks revered celestial gods, as well as other gods, that is, the chthonic gods. And those who were initiated in the Mysteries could truly be said to know the upper and the lower gods. The upper gods were those of Zeus's circle, but their rulership extended only to what is spread out before the senses, and what the human being can understand. But the human being is more than this. Part of the human being is rooted in the kingdom of the lower gods, in the kingdom of the chthonic gods.

But it is no good to look just at the parts of the human being illustrated in this sketch. If one is to take into account the rooting of the human being in the lower gods' kingdom, then one must complete the drawing to include the darkened moon (see drawing below).

In other words, one must regard the human head differently from the rest of the organism. With the rest of the organism one must be much more aware of the spiritual dimension, which is supersensible and invisible. As it faces us, the human head is externally complete. All that is spiritual has mirrored itself in the human head. This is not the case for the rest of the human being; the physical being is a mere fragment of the remaining part, and it is not enough to take this bodily fragment that wanders upon the earth.

All this shows that we must accept the human being's complexity. But do we encounter any of the things I just spoke about in real life? What I have just said seems abstract, paradoxical and hard to understand, yet the question must be asked: Does it ever come before us in real life? The important point is: it does appear in life, quite clearly so. The head is the instrument of our wisdom, so much so that our immediate wisdom is connected with its development. But even external anatomical or physiological observations—look how a head develops, how the human being grows up—show us that the head goes through a very different development from the rest of the organism. The head develops quickly, the rest of the organism slowly. For practical purposes, the head of the small child is already quite finished, it develops very little further. The rest of the organism is still little perfected and goes slowly through its stages. This is connected with the fact that in life as well we are really a twofold being. Not only does our skeleton divide into head and the remaining organism, life itself shows this twofold nature, in the rate of development of the head versus the rest of our organism. At the present time, the head develops practically up to our twenty-seventh or twenty-eighth year, the rest of the organism needs the whole of life until death to do so. In fact one needs a whole lifetime to experience what the head acquires relatively quickly. This is connected with many mysteries.

The spiritual investigator who witnesses a fatal accident has a special knowledge of these things—again, this sounds strange, but it expresses the full truth. Imagine that a person is struck down, dies in an accident. Let us suppose this person is thirty years old. To our physical observation such a death is some kind of accident, but from a spiritual outlook it is absurd to regard such an affair as accidental. For in the moment when from the outside, for some external cause, a person suddenly meets with death, a great deal happens very rapidly. Just think to yourselves: this same person who has been killed at the age of thirty would have become in the ordinary course of events perhaps seventy, eighty, ninety years old. If the person had lived from thirty to ninety, he or she would have gone through many life experiences, one after another. What thus would have been experienced in sixty years of life, the person now traverses rapidly, it might be in half a minute, when killed at the age of thirty. In the spiritual world, time relationships are quite different from what they seem to us here on the physical plane. A sudden death by accident can cause the experience, I say the experience, the life-wisdom, of a whole life that might still have been lived, to be passed through very rapidly.

In this way, we can see how a person assimilates life-wisdom, life-experience, throughout life. And we can use this to study the relationship between what the head, with its short development, can provide, and what the rest of the human being, with its long development in social life, can provide. It is true that during youth a person takes certain ideas and learns certain concepts; but the person only *learns* them. They are head knowledge. The rest of life runs more slowly, is destined to transform the head knowledge gradually into heart knowledge; knowledge in which the whole person shares, not just the head, I now call the whole person, heart-human.

We need much longer to transform head knowledge into heart knowledge than to assimilate head knowledge. Even if the head knowledge to be acquired is especially clever, one should be able to acquire it by one's twenties, wouldn't you say? Then one is a very clever person, academically speaking very clever. But in order to integrate this knowledge with one's whole being, one must remain flexible throughout one's life. And one needs as much longer to change head knowledge into heart knowledge as one lives beyond the twenty-sixth or twenty-seventh year. This is another way in which the human being is a twofold nature. Head knowledge is acquired quickly; and the course of life can change it into heart knowledge.

It is not easy to know what this signifies in practice. Perhaps I may venture to give an instance of the experience of spiritual investigators, suggesting that some things may be more easily known using their methods than other intellectual research. If one becomes acquainted with the language spoken by human beings who have gone through the gate of death and live in the spiritual world after death, if one understands the language of the dead, the so-called dead, one has the experience that the dead speak in very special ways about many things relating to human life. The dead have a language which we the living do not yet understand well. The understandings of the dead and the living lie somewhat far apart from one another today. The dead are thoroughly aware of the speed of development of the head-human, and the slowness of development of the heart-human. And if the dead wish to express what really happens when the rapidly acquired head knowledge transforms itself into the slower course of heart knowledge, they say that wisdom knowledge is transformed into heart warmth or love. Human wisdom is fructified as love. So speak the dead.

And that is in fact a profound and significant law of life. One can acquire head knowledge rapidly. It is possible to know a tremendous amount, particularly in our age, for natural science has made great strides in our time and is rich in content (although that is not always true of the natural scientists). But this content has remained cerebral knowledge, untransformed into heart knowledge because people, as I pointed out yesterday, no longer pay attention to what happens after the age of twenty-seven, because people no longer know how to grow old, or I should say, to remain young while growing old. Because they do not nurture the inner liveliness, their hearts grow cold; the heart warmth doesn't stream up to the head; love does not fructify the head. Head knowledge remains abstract theory. There is no necessity for it to remain cold theory, for all head knowledge has the potential to be transformed into heart knowledge. And that is precisely the task of the future: that head knowledge be gradually transformed into heart knowledge. A real miracle will take place when head knowledge is transformed into heart knowledge! Those who vigorously declaim against the materialistic natural sciences—or more precisely against the philosophy of nature (nineteenth-century *Naturphilosophie*)—are completely right, but at the same time something else is also true. Natural science has remained head knowledge in Haeckel, Spencer, Huxley, and so forth, and has turned into materialism; but if this natural knowledge became heart science, if it were absorbed by the whole human being, if humanity were to understand how to become old, or younger in old age, the science of today would indeed become spiritual, the true pursuit of the spirit and its existence. There is no better foundation than the natural science of today, if it is transformed into something that can flow to the head from the rest of the human organism, that is, from the spiritual part of the organism. The miracle will be complete when humans also learn to feel their rejuvenating etheric body so that the materialistic science of today will become spirituality. The more people find fault with its present materialism, its materialistic folly, the sooner nature science will become spirituality.

This will be linked to a complete transformation which can be felt by anyone with even the slightest feel for the present state of affairs; it will be linked with a complete transformation of all that has to do with education and instruction. Who would deny, given the social, moral, and historical conditions of the present time, that humanity as a whole is not in a position—and this sounds grotesque—to give children an adequate schooling, let alone an adequate education. We can make children into bureaucrats, industrialists, and even church ministers, but we are not really in any position to make children into complete human beings, well-developed, all-around human beings. This is the deep-seated need of our time; if the human being is to be an organism of soul and spirit developed in all its aspects, then that being must be able to transform throughout life what was absorbed hastily in childhood. The whole human being must remain fresh enough to keep transforming, throughout the course of life, what was absorbed.

For what do we really do in later life?—these things are not considered dispassionately enough—what do we really do? We have learned a certain amount in our youth, some more, some less; we are proud (aren't we, now?) that no illiterates are left in Western Europe. One person learns a lot, another learns less, but we all have learned something in our youth. And what do we do with this in later life, whether it was much or little? The way things are set up, we only remember the things we have learned; they are present in us in such a way that we can remember them. But how much do people work with these things? This learning has not been brought to the human soul in a form that remains active, so that head content can become heart content. It is not at all suited for that. A lot of water will have to flow down the Rhine before what we can give to the young now—I am talking about this one field, but it applies to all fields of endeavor—becomes suited to being transformed into heart knowledge. What is it that is needed? In fact, we have nothing at all today that could really undergo that process. For that, two conditions are lacking, and only rightly understood spiritual science can bring about these conditions.

Two conditions are lacking for really giving children something that renews life, something which, as long as they live, will be a source of joy and a support of life. Two things are missing. The first is that, from all the current ideas, all that modern culture can give us, people can attain no conception of their relationship with the universe. Just think of all that one is told in school. It is imparted even to the smallest children—at least what is being told is put in words that contain what I am describing to you. Reflect, if you will, that the human being grows up these days with the following ideas: there is the earth, it travels with such and such a velocity through universal space, and beyond the earth there are the sun, the planets, the fixed stars. And what is said of the sun, the stars, the planets is at most a kind of cosmic physics—it is no more really—cosmic mechanics. What the astronomer says today, what our culture generally says today about the structure of the universe, has that anything to do with this human being who walks here on earth? Most certainly not! Isn't it true that in the natural-scientific idea of the world, humans go about as a somewhat more highly developed animal? They are born, die, are buried, and so on. others come, are born, die, are buried, and so on, from generation to generation. Events take place out of the great cosmic space that can be calculated purely mathematically as if in a great machine. But for the modern intellectual, what has all that happens out there in the universe to do with the fact that here on earth this somewhat more highly developed animal is born and dies? Priests and pastors know no other wisdom to put in the place of this comfort-less wisdom. And since they do not know that, they say that they don't occupy themselves in any way with science, but that faith must have an entirely different origin.

Well, we need not expand on this. But two utterly differ-ent things are spoken of by atheistic science and by the so-called religious faith of this or that confession of the Church, feebly upholding the theistic side. It was essential that for a time in humanity's evolution the present world conception should take the place of earlier ideas. We need not go very far back—only people don't remember that today—to a time when humans were still aware that they did not wander on earth as higher animals who were just born and buried. Rather, they brought themselves into connection with the star world, with the whole universe, and knew in their own way, in a way very different from which must be striven for now, of their connection with the universe. But one must therefore conceive differently of the universe.

You see, a world conception like the one being imparted even to children today would have been unthinkable in the twelfth and thirteenth centuries; humans then could not in the least imagine having such an opinion of the world of the stars. They looked up to the stars and to the planets as we do today, but they did not merely calculate, as the mod-ern mathematical astronomer does, the orbits of the plan-ets, and believe that up there a globe was passing through world space—the science of the Middle Ages saw in each globe the body of a spiritual being. To represent a planet as a mere material globe would have been folly. Read about it in Thomas Aquinas. You will see everywhere that he sees an angelic intelligence in every planet. And likewise in the stars. There was no possibility of imagining a universe like the one modern astronomy has fabricated. But for a cer-tain time, in order to progress, the soul had to be driven, as it were, out of the universe, in order to conceive the skeletons, the pure machinery of the universe. Copernicus's, Galileo's, and Kepler's world conceptions had to come. But only the foolish see them as something valid for all times. They are a beginning, but a beginning that must evolve further.

Spiritual science knows many things already which official astronomy does not yet know. But it is important that just these things which spiritual science knows and official astronomy does not, should pass over into the general consciousness of humanity. And although these concepts may seem difficult today, the day will come when they will become something that we can impart to children, they will be an important possession of the children, to keep their souls full of life. For the time being, we still must speak of these things in difficult concepts. For as long as the spiritual is received by the world the way it is now, it has no opportunity to pour what is needed into the concepts and pictures to make these viable subjects of children's education.

There is one thing of which modern astronomy knows nothing. It knows nothing of the fact that the earth speeding through the universe is moving too fast. She rushes too fast, the earth! And rushing too fast, she speeds up the head development, making it quicker than it would be if the earth were moving at a rate corresponding to the duration of the whole human life. The rapidity of the development of the human head corresponds simply with the fact that the earth moves too quickly through universal space. Our head is caught up in this speed, but the rest of our organism is not; it is withdrawn from cosmic events. Our head, being a sphere, that is, an image of the heavens, must participate in the earth's performance in celestial space. But the rest of our organism, not being formed on the model of the universe, does not partake of its movement, and thus develops more slowly. If our whole organism were to participate in the speed of the earth, if it were to develop in concordance with the speed of the earth, none of us would live longer than twenty-seven years. Twenty-seven years would be the average length of a human life. For our head is finished when we turn twenty-seven; if it depended only on the head, the human being would die then. But the rest of the human being is planned to go on for a longer lifetime, and continually sends its forces into the head after our twenty-seventh year, making us live as long as we do. It is the spiritual part of the remaining organism which sends its forces to the head. It is the heart portion that shares its forces with the head.

If humanity knows someday that it has a twofold nature, a head nature and a heart nature, it will know then that the head obeys quite different cosmic laws than the rest of the organism. Humanity will take its place again within the macrocosm, then the human being will unfailingly develop concepts to recognize: "I do not stand on earth merely as a higher animal, to be born and die; I am a being formed out of the whole universe. My head is built up for me out of the whole universe; the earth has attached it to the rest of my organism which does not follow the cosmos as my head does." Thus, when we look at the human being not as an abstraction, as modern science does, but as a dual being, head-human and heart-human, in connection with the universe, then the human being is placed again into the cosmos. And I know, and others who can judge these things know: once human beings can form heart-warm concepts of the fact that looking at the human head one sees an image of the whole star-strewn space of the world with its wonders, then all the pictures of the connection between the human being and the wide,wide universe will enter the human soul. And these pictures will become forms of narrative which we do not yet have, and which will bring to expression, not abstractly but with feeling, what can be poured into the hearts of young children. And the young children's hearts will feel: Here I stand upon the earth, a human being, and as such the expression of the whole star-strewn universal space; the whole world is expressed in me. It will be possible to train the human being to feel like a member of the whole cosmos.

The second necessary condition is that we must organize education in such a way that human beings know they are images of the universe in their head, and separate from the universe in the rest of their organism. Then they will know that, with the rest of their organism, they must work upon what falls down like a rain of the soul—the whole universe—so that it will become independent in the human being on earth. And this will be a very special inner experience. Think of this twofold human being, which I will now draw in this curious fashion.

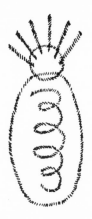

Once we know that the secrets of the stars flow from the whole universe into the human head, stimulating its forces, and that for a lifetime this must be worked upon by the rest of the organism so that it may be conserved on earth, and then carried through death into the spiritual world— that is, once science becomes a living experience—then humans will know their twofold nature, they will know themselves as head-human and heart-human. For what I am saying now means that human beings will learn to solve their own riddle, to say to themselves: Inasmuch as I become more and more heart-human, inasmuch as I remain young, then in my later years I will view through my heart forces what I learned with my head as a child and youth. The heart gazes up to the head and sees there an image of the whole starry heavens. The head will look to the heart and find there the mysteries of the human riddle, will learn to fathom in the heart the actual essence of the human being. When it comes to education, human beings will feel: Yes, I can learn all sorts of things. But as I go on living, as I live on toward death that will bear me into the spiritual world, what I learn in my head will be fructified in the future through the love ascending from the rest of the organism and will be transformed. There is something in me as a human being that is only to be found in me as a human being. I have to wait for that something. I shall be thirty, forty, fifty, sixty years old, and as I grow from decade to decade, something of the mystery of humanity comes toward me through the mere fact of growing older. I have something to await from the mere fact of living on.

Imagine if that were not mere theory, but instead life-theory, social life-wisdom. The child would then be educated in such a way that it would know: "I can learn something; the person who teaches me possesses something that I cannot learn; before finding it in myself I must become as old as this person. When I hear something from my teacher, I am receiving something that must be a sacred mystery, since I can hear it from this person's mouth, but can't find it in myself." Just think what a relationship is created between children and their elders, which is entirely lost in our age, when people know that aging offers something worth awaiting. If I am not yet forty years old, the sum of mysteries cannot lie in me that can lie in a person more than forty years old. And if it is imparted to me, I receive it as just information; I cannot know it in my innermost being. What a bond of human fellowship would be formed if in this way a new earnestness, a new profundity came into life!

This earnestness, this depth, is precisely what is lacking from our life, what our life does not have. Our present life values only head knowledge. But true social life will die out this way; it will dissolve, for on this earth human beings wander about without any idea who they are. They really take seriously only whatever happens till the age of twenty-seven and then spend the remainder of their lives carrying the corpse around in them, not transforming into the human being what can remain youthful through death.

Because people do not understand this, because we live in an age that cannot understand this, everything that has to do with the spiritual remains unsatisfying, as I said yesterday concerning Friedrich Schlegel. He was a gifted man, he had understood much, but he didn't know that a new revelation was needed; he thought he could just simply take the old Christianity. In many respects he could say the right things in ringing words: I will read you a passage from his last lecture in the year 1828. He sought to prove, as he said, "that in the course of world history a divine guiding hand and disposition is to be recognized, that no merely earthly visible forces are cooperating in this evolution, or opposing or hindering it, but that the conflict is directed in part under divine assistance against invisible powers. I hope to have established my conviction of this, even though it is not mathematically proven, which would be neither proper nor feasible, and that it will nevertheless remain active and vigorous."

He had a presentiment, but not a living consciousness, that human beings, by living through history, had to become familiar in history with divine forces, and together with these divine forces fight against opposing spiritual powers—he says expressly "opposing spiritual powers." For in certain respects, people flee from the real science of the spirit. Since the third century of our era, when in the West the prejudice, as it was called, arose against the "persuasion of the false gnosis" (that was what they called it!), people have gradually turned aside from all that is knowable about the spiritual worlds. And so it came about that even religious impulses paved the road for materialism, and that these religious impulses could not prevent the fact that we have really nothing to give to youth. Our science does not serve the young. In later life, we can merely remember the things it taught; it cannot become heart-wisdom.

It is the same in the religious field. Humanity has come, it seems, to two extremes. Humanity seems to have forgotten how to conceive of the supersensible Christ and has no desire to know anything of that cosmic power of which spiritual science must speak again as the power of Christ Jesus. On the other hand, quite delightful, really lovely and charming pictures were developed around the Infant Jesus in the Middle Ages and in modern times through the medium of poetry and music. But pictures and ideas related to the dear Jesus child cannot satisfy a religious person for a whole life! It is in fact characteristic that a paradoxical love for the sweet little Jesus is expressed in countless songs and so on. It is not objectionable as such, but there has to be more.

That is the one area where humans, in order to have at least something, have clung to the smallest, since they cannot raise themselves to the great. But it cannot fill up life. And on the other hand, we have the *bon Dieu citoyen* as we learned to know him in Heinrich Heine's words, the "good citizen" Jesus who is divested of all divinity, the God of liberal pastors and priests. Now do you really believe that this being can take a hold on life? Do you believe in particular that he can captivate young people? He is from the very outset the product of a dead theology, not even theology, but rather a product of theological history. In this sphere, however, people are far from directing their gaze to what is really spiritual power in history.

Why is this so? Very simply, for a time humankind must go through a stage of gazing into the world from a purely materialistic standpoint. The time has come when modern natural science, which is so fitted for spirituality, must be transformed into heart knowledge. Our natural science will be either execrable, if it remains as it is now, or else it will be something extraordinarily grand, if it changes into heart knowledge. For then it becomes spiritual science. The older science, which is still incorporated in traditions, had already worked for that transformation of head knowledge into heart knowledge; the modern age has not yet had a gift for transforming in that way what it has acquired, until now. And so, especially in the social sciences, head science has produced the only real work, and therefore the most one-sided work conceivable.

The human head cannot know anything of the being of the person. Hence when the head ponders over the human being and its involvement in social life, it must bring something quite foreign into social life. That is modern socialism, in its form of social democratic theory. Nothing is quite as pure head knowledge as the Marxist social democracy. This is only because the rest of the world has rejected any concern with world problems, while Marxist circles have occupied themselves only with social theories. The others have—no, I will be polite—let themselves be dominated only by professorial, that is, purely conservative, thoughts. But head wisdom has become social theory. That is to say, people have tried to build a social theory with the instrument least suited for knowing anything

about the human being. This is a fundamental error of
present-day humanity, the extent of which will not be fully
revealed until people understand the matter of head versus heart knowledge. The head will never be able to refute
socialism, Marxist socialism, because in our time the
head's task is to think and make plans. It will be refuted
only by spiritual science, since spiritual science is head wisdom transformed through the heart.

To understand these things is of the utmost importance.
You see now why even a man like Schlegel suggested
unsuitable means—since he was willing to accept the old,
although he realized that we must recapture a vision of the
invisible residing among us. But our age has a challenge to
direct the gaze to the invisible. Invisible powers were always
at hand, as Schlegel divined; unseen powers have taken
part in working upon what is accomplished in humankind.
But humanity must evolve. Up to a certain point, it did not
matter much if people in the last few centuries gave little
thought to the supersensible, invisible forces, for instance
in social life. But that will no longer do in the future. In the
future, dealing with the real conditions, that won't do! I
could give quite a few examples to show this; I will bring
one forward.

In the course of the last decade and a half, I have spoken of this in other contexts. Any observer of the social
state of Europe as it has developed since the eighth century knows that many different things have affected the
structure of European life, this complex European life.
The West has retained Athanasian Christianity and thrust
back eastward an older Christianity, originally linked with
Asiatic traditions, the Russian Christianity, Orthodox
Christianity. In the West, Athanasian Christianity, by form-
ing progressively an articulated organism out of the preserved Roman element together with the newly revived
German and Slav elements, created the various members

of this complex organism, the European social entity. Until now, it was possible to operate in that complex organism by disregarding what lives there unseen, for there is much strength in the structure of the configuration we call Europe. An essential and important force in this structure, among others, is the relation between France and the rest of Europe. I do not mean merely political relations; I mean the whole relation of France with the rest of Europe, and by this I mean all that any European could have felt in the course of centuries, since the eighth and ninth centuries, with regard to anyone belonging to the French nation. The peculiarity is that the relation of Europe to France is expressed as sympathy or antipathy. In dealing with sympathy or antipathy, we are dealing with a phenomenon of a purely physical nature. If we study what hearts, what human souls live on the physical plane, we can understand the human relationship between France and the rest of Europe. What has developed for France is to be understood through physical conditions. Hence it did no harm—there were similar relationships all over Europe in the last centuries—if people neglected the way supersensible powers play into things, since the sympathies and antipathies were caused by purely physical factors.

Much of all this will become different. We are standing before powerful revolutions (even in regard to intimate relations) that will overcome the European social structure. You should not take it lightly if I say once again that things should be taken more earnestly than people nowadays are inclined to take them. We are standing before mighty revolutions, and human beings of the future will have to turn their eyes—the eyes of the mind—to spiritual relationships, for physical relations will no longer suffice to explain what is going on. Events can be understood only by taking spiritual relations into consideration.

What took place in March—the fall of the Czar—has a metaphysical quality; it can be understood only if one has in mind that metaphysical character. Why then was there a Czar at all? The question can be answered in a higher sense than the external trivial historical sense. Why was there a Czar at all? If one disregards individual pacifistic cranks who took seriously the tomfoolery of the Czar's peace manifesto, one must say squarely: Even those who, for a range of reasons, sided with the Russian realm, even they have not loved czardom. And in those who did love it, the love was certainly not genuine. So why was there czardom? There was czardom—I will say it paradoxically, even extremely—so that Europe had something to hate. It was necessary to provoke those forces of hatred. Europe needed this hate as a sort of fresh impetus to something new. The Czar must be there, in the first place, to serve as the point on which hatred concentrated; for a wave of hatred was prepared, and it can be observed in external manifestations. What is being prepared now will be transformed into powerful feelings of hatred. It will no longer be possible to understand these as the sympathy and antipathy of former times were to be understood. Hatred will come not just from human beings. Central and Eastern Europe will be hated, not by human beings, but by certain demons that will dwell in human bodies. The time will come when Eastern Europe will be hated even more than Central Europe.

These things must be understood, and they cannot be taken lightly. They can be understood only if human beings lift themselves to see a connection with the spiritual world. For what was already to some extent divined by spirits like Friedrich Schlegel will come to pass, though those spirits did not see the foundations and the roots. Things must be seen dispassionately in the eye of the soul, so that human beings can look back over the past centuries and what they have wrought. Then they will be able to cooperate in the foundation of the future.

Among the fine passages that occur from time to time in Schlegel's addresses is this: "In the evolution of humanity, all depends on the inner being of the soul and on sincerity in the soul; most harmful is every kind of political idolatry." How this political idolatry has laid hold of our time! How it rules our time! And this political idolatry has created its own symptom by which one is able to recognize its presence.

But one must unravel the connections. One must feel what is living in our time. Unless we deepen knowledge of the heart, we have no chance of giving children what they need to keep young and fit for life all life through. We do not as yet have this possibility.[1] But it must be created, something must happen. We can say, summarizing things in a few words: Schoolmastering is unable to perform its mission. Schoolmastering is completely foreign to the true being of humanity. But the world threatens to be ruled by a schoolmaster who is the object of idolatrous veneration.[2] Schoolmasters, the least fitted to guide humanity in the modern epoch, will play high politics.

Some people at least should understand these things. For they are things with a profound connection to the deep knowledge that humanity can gain only by seeking to penetrate the secrets of the human being. The world today can neither be understood nor in any way governed through desires and instincts, through chauvinism and nationalism, but solely through the good will which tries to penetrate true reality.

---

1. The first Waldorf school was not founded until 1919.
2. Woodrow Wilson.

13 January 1918

WE HAVE SEEN that when we begin to observe the human being, we approach some riddles of the universe, since we can see in the human being's twofold form something of the solution of the world riddle. Meditating about all these things, we are helped by the formula: The world as a totality is a riddle, and the human being, also taken as a totality, is its solution. We must not, however, expect to solve the world riddle in a moment; human life itself in its entirety, what we experience between birth and death and again between death and birth—that is the solution of the world riddle. So this is a very serviceable formula: The world is a riddle, and the human being is its solution.

We have seen that, when we regard the external human physical form, we can distinguish between the head part and the remaining part. We can consider the head part in its spherical form as an image of the whole cosmos, not just by way of comparison but in actuality. We can truly say that the whole starry heaven is involved in bringing about the form, the shaping, the inner forces of the human head. Of course, it is also true, speaking lightly, that everyone has a unique head; certainly each human being does. For, as you know, the configuration of the place and time of a person's birth results in each person having a unique head according to the position of the stars in the heavens. Let us keep in mind that our head is not built up by the starry heaven in general, but by its specific configuration. And from various studies, we realize that a considerable part of the human being's task between death and rebirth is to become familiar with the mysteries, the spiritual secrets of the stars. One can even say that, in a certain sense, the head is not given us passively, but that we make it ourselves. Between death and the next birth, we come to know all the laws that prevail in wide cosmic space. In fact, when we think of it spiritually, the wide universe is our home between death and a new birth. And just as here on earth we learn to know the laws by which houses and other things are constructed, so in the time between death and rebirth we become familiar with the laws of the cosmos. And from the cosmos, together with the purely spiritual beings who dwell there, we work chiefly upon the head. So when the human head appears in the physical world, it only appears to be determined solely by heredity from one's ancestors. I have said repeatedly that everyone acknowledges that the magnetic pole of the needle does not turn by itself to the North and the other pole to the South, but that cosmic forces are at work, namely, that the earth is exercising its influence. In the case of the magnet, people admit that the universe plays a part, but when we come to the origin of the human being they are not yet willing to acknowledge that the whole universe participates. In the case of the human being, the whole universe is concerned with the formation of the head. The head has not merely been shaped by heredity from father, mother, grandparents, and so on, but by forces from the whole universe acting within it. Principally through the limbs and members, the configuration of cosmic forces acts upon the content of the head. On the other hand, insofar as the rest of our organism is physical, we do receive it, through a kind of hereditary transmission, from generations of ancestors.

Modern natural science is very close to discovering this from its own standpoint. Actually, the natural science of today combats only those parts of the truth that are suggestive of spiritual science. But a meeting between natural and spiritual science is very near on many points. I have said in other lectures and indicated here that natural science is on the verge of discovering something that has met with skepticism even in spiritual circles. People who read my *Theosophy* find themselves repelled by the chapter about the human aura, by the way an individual's forces of soul and spirit are expressed for clairvoyants in a color aura that sparkles around them. Professor Moritz Benedikt, whom I have often mentioned in other connections, has recently made experiments in Vienna with gifted dowsers. Professor Benedikt did not make experiments about clairvoyance since he is not the least bit interested in acknowledging clairvoyance, but he has made experiments in a dark room with gifted dowsers, who have played such an important role in this war. Since water was needed for soldiers, people with a gift for using divining rods were assigned to various army units, especially in the southern battle zones, to help find water. Of course, driven by necessity, one had to do such things. Now in the camera obscura and with the methods of natural science, Professor Benedikt has examined people who can find water or metals under the earth by means of the divining rod. In the case of one woman who was quite small, Benedict discovered that treatment in the camera obscura showed her to have an immense aura, so immense that she looked like a giant. Benedikt could even describe the right side as bluish, the left side as yellowish red. This can all be read today as scientific findings, since Professor Benedikt has published the whole matter in his book on the divining rod. What has been observed by Professor Benedikt is the aura. It is not the aura as we understand it; we mean by the word much more spiritual elements than this most inferior, almost physical, aura which Professor Benedikt is able to find by natural means in the camera obscura. Still there is a connection. Precisely that part of my book *Theosophy* which has met with the most opposition and abuse has thus been found to have points of contact with ordinary science. Things will move quickly.

It will be the same with regard to the matters I have just touched upon. In a short time, and based purely on natural scientific research, it will be possible to establish that what an individuality bears within itself as inherited from ancestors is not the form of the head, and not the head's inner forces, and that the head is in fact produced by forces in the cosmos. If we went by our heads alone, we should never be nationalistic. The head is not in the least fitted for nationalism, for it is derived from the heavens, and the heavens are not nationalistic. Any division into groups does not come from the head; it comes from that element through which we are connected with the hereditary stream of humanity. This of course plays into the head when the human being lives here between birth and death, for the rest of the organism is continuously exchanging its nerve forces and its blood forces with the head.

When we speak of heredity, however, and say that the other ("non-head") part of the human being received its force from the ancestors, we must refer only to the physical element, for the spiritual aspects of that remaining organism are another matter again. It is very important, therefore, for us to consider a fact which can be brought to light only through spiritual science. Natural science will discover, as it has discovered the aura, that the head is influenced through heredity only by being attached to the rest of the organism. That people are only related to their ancestors by other parts of their organism, this too will be discovered by natural science. But we touch here upon another field which natural science cannot enter forthwith.

Inasmuch as we are born, we bear in our head the forces of the universe: they shape our head. A little of that, to be sure, can be substantiated outwardly. Anyone who observes children's development will perhaps know that, in the very early days, people often ask whom the child resembles; and the likeness often only comes out strongly in later childhood. Some of you will have noticed that. This is due to the fact that the head is mainly neutral as regards earth conditions. The rest of the organism must first affect the head (which of course can happen already at the embryonic stage), and then the features and so on may show a likeness to the ancestors.

If one has any feeling for such things, it is possible to see externally the truth of this. But the matter goes deeper. Between the spiritual universe—for the universe is filled with spirit and spirit beings—and the earth on which we dwell, is a restless go-between. A subtle substance, which cannot be produced in the chemistry lab since it does not belong to the chemical elements, streams in continuously onto the earth out of the universe. If one wants to think of it schematically, one can say: The earth is here in universal space, universal matter continuously streams in from all sides toward the earth, a fine universal substance (arrows inward) that even penetrates a little below the earth's surface.

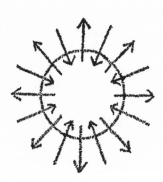

So this continually takes place—substances from the whole of cosmic space rain down toward the earth. It is not physical substance, not a chemical element, but actually spiritual, auric substance that sinks down below the surface of the earth. When we come down to earth from the spiritual world to find a place in a human body, we use the forces that lie in this substance.

Now it is significant that this substance streaming into the earth and out again is used by the human being at death. The human being uses this substance in order to regain its forces prior to returning to the spiritual world. This substance, which I have shown coming inward toward the earth, enters the surface to a certain depth and then streams out again (arrows outward). So one can actually perceive a sort of inhalation of ether or auric substance into the earth, and again an exhalation.

The following observation is not very easy to make. But if one has observed it once, if one has realized that the earth actually inhales and exhales spiritual substance continuously, then one knows how to apply it in all circumstances, and above all to human life in the way I have just described. Thus we come into our bodily nature with what I have drawn as inwardly directed arrows, and we pass out in death with those pointing outward.

In this case, I will point out how I came upon this fact years ago. The forces that play here, the inflow and outflow of forces, are not concerned solely with human life, but with every possible kind of earthly condition. The problem for me was how matters stood with cockchafers—yes cockchafers, of all things. Actually, cockchafers are extraordinarily interesting because, as you may know, when there are many cockchafers in a year, then three or five years later there are very many grubs—their larvae. These larvae affect the potato crops very seriously; many grubs means a very bad crop. Anyone who has anything to do with potato culture knows that there will be a bad crop three or five years after a year in which there are many cockchafers. I had looked into that as an interesting fact, and then I discovered that the life of the cockchafers is connected with the substance flowing in and the life of the grub with the substance flowing out. I only stress this as a way of showing you how one comes upon things from very different angles. One is most certain to come upon things when one is not observing something as the direct object of one's attention but as a relatively indifferent object, toward which one can most easily maintain a neutral attitude. You see, however, that the substances of which I have spoken penetrate the earth and remain there for a while. The substance that streams in one year only streams out several years later. This is also connected with the fact that the substance flowing out is on the whole heavier than the substance flowing in. The latter is more active, streams in faster; the substance streaming out is heavier and flows more slowly.

Intensive observation of human life shows how the human being uses the forces of the incoming substance when emerging from the universe at birth. In subsequent years, the connection is lost. You will have realized from what I have said that it is the head which is chiefly affected by the substances flowing in. But the human head is a hard globe. It is indeed a hard globe, and of all the organs the most ossified. Thus, the head loses its connections with the inflowing forces relatively early, not in childhood, but relatively early. Hence its formation and development are finished early.

The human being remains connected with these forces throughout childhood, and then they cease influencing the person, at least in our cosmic cycle. It was not always so on earth, as I will come to presently, but it is so now. Now while the person lives here on earth, the rest of the organism, that is, the part that is not the head, takes possession of the substances flowing out and of their forces. The remaining part of the organism imbues itself with them, and these are the forces which help the organism's rejuvenation from without, as I indicated yesterday. They are the rejuvenating forces that act upon the etheric body and make the etheric more and more chubby-faced while we are growing old physically. In case people wonder what I mean by chubby-faced, I will remark that the cheeks of children have the rounded quality that we see, for instance, on the faces of musician angels in pictures. In other words, to the extent that the human being is an etheric being, it grows a round, chubby child's face. In this process undergone by the etheric body in connection with the remaining organism, the forces streaming out of the earth are operative. And it is these same forces which we use when we go through the portal of death to return to the cosmos, the spiritual world.

The earth, as you see, has a share in our life, is inwardly involved in it. And something else yet is connected with it, which can very easily be made into a formula—an important, essential formula. We live for a long time as souls between death and rebirth, before entering the physical world again through birth, and we live as souls again after passing through the portal of death to return to the cosmos, to the spiritual world, until our next incarnation. The dead live a spiritual life, and this life is connected with the stars, just as here on earth we are connected with physical matter. Since our head has been formed and shaped by the forces that influenced us between death and new birth, since we built our head, as it were, out of cosmic forces, our own real being of soul and spirit finds its spiritual grave in our head relatively early. We possess the head forces that we have here on earth because our head is actually the grave of our soul life as we led it before birth, or before conception. Our head is the grave of our spiritual existence. But inasmuch as we have come down to earth, the rest of our organism is used to resurrect us, for it takes up the forces which stream from the earth into universal space, in order to form its spiritual element. And while our physical organism falls away from us, our spiritual part with our forces that stream out from the earth, passes through cosmic space into spirit existence.

This is the wonderful polarity that prevails in the universe regarding the human being. We became physical out of the spirit, burying our spirit nature in the head; the head is the end of our spiritual existence before birth. Here upon earth it is reversed. We leave the physical behind; the physical disintegrates gradually during our life, and the spiritual arises. Therefore we can say that birth denotes the resurrection of the physical, the spiritual being changed into the physical, while death denotes the birth of the spiritual, the physical being given over to the earth, just as the spiritual is handed over to the universe at our birth. We give our spiritual element to the universe by being born, and by dying we hand over to the universe our physical element. By giving our spiritual part to the universe, we are physical human beings. By giving our physical part to the earth through death, we are spiritual human beings in the period between death and a new birth. That is the polarity, the contrast. And our life here consists in developing our spirit organism. But we can develop it in the right way for our present earthly cycle only when what I said yesterday is taken into consideration. That is to say, when we reach the point where both members of human nature enter into correspondence with one another, when head life and heart life enter into correspondence with one another, and the shorter head life really stretches itself out by coming to life in the whole being. Thus the whole human being can be rejuvenated during the lifetime, when in fact the head has long since lost its mobility, its power of inner development.

The special task of future pedagogy will be to make anthroposophical spiritual science so fruitful that people come to feel how we are built up out of the cosmos, how the person literally peels off from the cosmos and gives back to the cosmos what was acquired on earth. This education must be imparted through all sorts of narratives, all sorts of things which are adapted to young people, but so adapted that one can retain one's interest for the things learned through every age of life. I ask of you only, not to think through, for that is not much use, but to feel through, thoroughly to feel through, one thing. Here too, you see, is a point where modern natural science is already concerning itself with the matters investigated by spiritual science. I have mentioned how intelligent geologists have expressed the view that the earth is already dying out. The earth has already passed its midlife as earthbeing. In the excellent book by Eduard Suess, *The Face of the Earth*, the purely materialistic geologist Suess states that when one walks over fields today and looks at the clods of earth, one is dealing with something that is dying out, that was once thriving. It is dying, the earth is dying. We know this from spiritual science, since we know that the earth will be translated into another planetary existence, which we call the Jupiter existence. Thus the earth as such is dying away. But the human being, that is, the human race as sum of spiritual beings, does not die with the earth; humanity lives beyond the earth, as it has lived before the earth was Earth, as I described in my *Occult Science*. And so, one can permeate oneself with the feeling—again not the thought, but the feeling, the experience—with the conception, "I stand here on this earthly soil, but the ground on which I stand, in which I shall find my grave, has but a short appearance in the cosmos."

How then does a next earth, a new planet arise out of this earth and how can a new humanity of the future

dwell on it? How does it arise? It arises through the fact
that we ourselves, piece by piece, carry what is needed to
form this new planetary existence. We human beings (the
animal kingdom is also involved to some extent) inasmuch as we always carry within us something belonging to
the next life, are already, here and now, in the course of
this our physical life, preparing the next planet that will
follow the earth's existence. What is to be the future of
the earth resides in the forces that return to the cosmos.
We do not live merely in the present; we live in the future
of the earth, but we have to keep returning into incarnation to complete unfinished business on earth, as long as
earth exists. But we are involved in the future life of the
earth. We have said that the earth breathes spirit substance. In the substances that are breathed in, we carry
the past, the laws of the past, the forces of the past. In
what is breathed out, given back, we bear what belongs to
the future. In the human race itself lies the future of
earth's existence.

Think of all this in a really fecund way, with feeling and
warmth, instead of all the stupid drivel which is imparted to
the young these days; think of this brought to life in hundreds and hundreds of vivid narrations and parables, and
brought to the young! Think what a feeling toward the universe would be aroused—what there is to do! What there is
to be done if our civilization is to go forward, how much
there is to do concretely! This is very important. And it can
be considered all the more so since it is connected with
what I called the rejuvenation of the human being. The fact
that present humanity has come to such a calamitous pass is
connected with the fact that it has lost the secret of chang-
ing head life into heart life. We have hardly any real heart
life. What people generally speak of as such is the life of
instincts and desires, merely that, not the spiritual element
of which I have spoken. Today, people allow whatever is

streaming out of the earth to just stream out; they don't bother themselves about it. They pay no attention.

Some individuals instinctively are concerned. I recently gave an example of the different ways in which individuals take things into account. I related the example of Professors Zeller and Michelet. I said that I spoke with Eduard von Hartmann about the two men, just when Zeller had obtained his pension, no longer feeling able, at seventy-two, to hold his lectures at the university. But Michelet was ninety-three years old, and Hartmann related that Michelet had just been there and told Hartmann, "I don't understand Zeller, who is only seventy-two and saying he cannot go on lecturing. I am ready to lecture for another ten years." And with that Michelet skipped about the room and gleefully planned what he would lecture about the next year, and couldn't imagine how that lad Zeller, the seventy-two-year-old Zeller, could have put in a claim to be pensioned off.

This keeping young is connected with exchanges between the head and the heart. This can happen in single individuals, but on the whole, it can occur even in single individuals only if it becomes part of our whole civilization, if our whole cultural life becomes imbued with the principle that it should have not just head life, but heart life as well. But you see, to acquire heart life requires more patience. Despite the fact that it is more creative, more youth-giving, still heart life requires more patience. Head life...well, one sits down and crams. And when we are young we prefer to stick to our cramming despite all our teachers' admonitions. For some customs have survived from the ancient past, when things were still known out of atavism, but people no longer know how to interpret these customs. I shall remind you of one.

All the things that have been preserved from the relatively recent past, before materialism had become generalized, have a deeper meaning. For instance, in recent decades the habit has been lost, but when I was young (it is some time ago) there was an arrangement in the Grammar School—in the Lower School it was in the second class—to have Ancient History, and then in the fifth class one had Ancient History again. Those who planned these regulations at that time no longer knew why it was so, and the teachers did not act as if they knew the reasons for it either. But any aware person would have said "When I give history to a boy in the second class, he crams it, but what he takes in needs a few years for it to be at home in his organism. Therefore it is a good thing to give the same things again in the fifth class, for only then does the knowledge that entered his poor head three or four years ago bear its good fruit." The whole structure of the old Grammar School was really built up on these things. The monastic schools of the Middle Ages still had many traditions derived from ancient wisdom, a wisdom that is not ours, but one that, preserved as an atavism from the ancient past, arranges these things logically.

In fact, the principle of patience is needed if the life of the head is to pass over into the life of the heart. For while head life unites quickly with us, heart life moves more slowly; it is less active, so we must wait. Today people like to understand everything at once. Just imagine if a person decided to learn something and then had to wait a few years in order to fully understand it. Such a principle can hardly be related to the frame of mind of people today. The feelings of modern people run along very different lines.

Let me point out some examples of this. Lately, two plays were produced in Zurich by people connected with the Anthroposophical Society. In fact, it has been widely pointed out that the two people are connected with the building in Dornach, spiritual science, and so on. In this case, to be quite just, it must be acknowledged that two

Zurich performances by Pulver and Reinhart have been really well received in Switzerland. But one can find remarkable things in the correspondence that has gone out of Switzerland. The foreign correspondents have shown themselves, well, less interested, shall we say, than the Swiss audiences themselves. Thus I have had a newspaper given to me in which these first two Swiss performances by Pulver and Reinhart were discussed. The correspondent cannot resist pointing out that the two authors are connected with our movement and have drawn a great deal from it. Presently, people are not only afraid of the wrong teaching of the Gnosis, as I related yesterday, they are afraid of anything concerning the life of the spirit. If something about world conception creeps into anything—oh! how dreadful! And this actually rests upon the fact that there is no feeling for this relation of head life and heart life. All the life to be found in humanity today outside the head is purely the life of instinct and desire; it is not spiritual. And so the life of instinct and desire is irritated with the mere head life. Head life these days is very spiritual, very intellectual, but it will become more and more contaminated by instincts and desire. Hence thoughts come forth in a curious fashion. And this correspondent of whom I speak—you can perhaps best judge the confusion of his head through his instincts if I read you a characteristic sentence showing his fears that questions about worldviews come into the plays of the two authors. Just think, the man goes so far as to write:

> But Pulver's belief in Christ ought to grow out of depths of sorrow and doubt if he wished to win disciples from the stage. The star flower plucked by Reinhart's seeker after Paradise at his studio window in the very first scene ought to bloom only at the end and from a bleeding heart.

And now comes the sentence I had in mind:

Both poets' worldview was already complete in their heads as they began to write; it would have been better for the dramas if they had to wrestle for their religion as they wrote.

Now just think of that; today it is considered a serious fault for someone to have a world conception when sitting down to write! One is supposed to sit down as a perfect fool in face of the world and scribble away, and then in the scribbling, at the end, a world conception is supposed to spring forth. Then the thing is produced at the theater, and this is supposed to please the audience! Just imagine such stupid nonsense being actually spread abroad in the world today; and many people do not notice that such rubbish is being circulated.

Such things depend simply on the fact that the life of the head is not worked on by the whole being. For of course, the journalist who wrote that was a very "clever man." That should not be disputed. He was very clever. But it is of no possible use to be clever, if the cleverness is mere head life. That is the important thing to keep in mind; it is extraordinarily important.

Here we touch upon something very fundamental, very necessary to our present civilization. One can observe similar things at every turn. Logical slips are not made today because people lack logic, but because logic is not enough. One can be wonderfully logical, pass examinations splendidly, be a brilliant professor of national economy or any other subject, and, in spite of being so clever and having any amount of logic to spare, one can nevertheless go off the rails again and again; one will fail to accomplish anything connected with real life if one doesn't have the patience to integrate into one's whole being what is grasped by the head, if one doesn't have the patience to call upon the rejuvenating forces in human nature. That is the whole point. Those having anything to do with true science, such as spiritual science, know that they would be ashamed to give a lecture tomorrow on what they found out and learned today—because they know that it would be absolutely valueless. Its value would emerge only years afterwards. The conscientious spiritual investigator cannot lecture by giving out what has been only just learned; but things must be kept continually present to the soul so that they may ripen. If what has only just been acquired is brought forward, at least special reference should be made to the fact, so that the audience may note it. One will really be able to see what the present time needs only if one bears in mind these demands of human nature. For what is necessary for the present age does not lie where people mostly seek it; it lies in more subtle structures that nevertheless are present everywhere. Without going into politics, here is one example that deserves attention.

Many people today—more than is good for the world at any rate—are of the opinion that this war must continue as long as possible, so that from it general peace may arise. If it ends too quickly, they say, it does peace no service. I am passing no judgment on the value or lack of value of the so-called peace negotiations between the Central Powers and Russia, but it has been interesting all the same in the last few days to see what curious kind of logic can be worked out. I have been given an extraordinarily interesting article on this matter. The gentleman in question (his name is of no consequence) argues against a so-called separate peace because he considers that it would not further universal peace. A direct way of thinking—but one perhaps that would require one to dig a little deeper, might rather say, "Well, we might make a certain amount of progress if at least in one spot on earth we stopped mowing each other down." That would be a straightforward way of thinking. A less direct way of thinking comes out as follows: "No, one really may not stop fighting in one place, for in that way universal peace would not be promoted." And now the gentleman in question goes into interesting explanations, that is, explanations that interest him, as to how people quarrel over words. It is his opinion that the people who say, "One should be enthusiastic about any peace, even if it is a separate peace," are hypnotized by words. But one must not be dependent on words; one must go to the core of the matter, and the matter is just this—that a separate peace is harmful to the general peace of the world. Among the various arguments adduced by the gentleman are the following very interesting sentences, most characteristic for the present day. Where shall I begin?, I don't want to become too personal. Anyway, as he puts it: "Any honest person must admit that this is the motive of many (not all!) among us who so delight in a separate peace, and in Lenin and Trotsky, [he means that enthusiasm for the *word* peace is the motive] while at the same time tirelessly shouting down the antimilitarists and showing little appreciation for our own Lenins and Trotskys. We however who are not duped by words but want to get at the core of the matter, we do not want simply a German peace, but peace, we want general peace. For us the word 'separate' is in contradiction with the word 'peace'." If one takes the article seriously, we are being asked seriously to distinguish between peace and peace! And the article is headed "Peace and Peace."

Then the gentleman, who spends the whole article excoriating those who worship a word, writes the following:

> ... for us the word "separate" stands in contradiction to the word "peace." Separation is the principle of strife, not the principle of peace. After this World-War, we need a World-Peace in which all nations

reach at the same time a great mutual agreement. What we see in Brest-Litovsk, this game of a select circle of diplomats, imbued with all the subtleties of diplomacy, with the naivete, the idealism (and the dogmatism) of the representatives of a new order, is a spectacle that can please no one who wishes the ideal to remain pure. It is to be feared that we may get a Devil's peace, which will only lead to more frightful war, instead of God's peace which finally leads to an end to all war.

Well, this is certainly logical, for the article is written with great ingenuity; it is brilliantly ingenious. This article "Peace and Peace" is even boldly and courageously written because it flies in the face of the prejudice of countless people, but its logic is devoid of any connection with reality. For the connection with reality is found only through what we have spoken of, the maturing of knowledge; what the head can experience must be reflected upon in the rest of the person and must mature. It is safe to say that what the very clever people of today lack most of all is this ripening. This lack is connected with the deepest needs and impulses of the present. You see, the present has no inclination at all to study these things. Naturally, I do not mean that every single person can go in for such a study, but people whose metier it is to study ought to occupy themselves with these things, and then that would communicate to the rest of humanity. For isn't it true, with all due respect, that journalists write what they find to be the general opinion?

If, instead of Wilsonianism or some such thing, Islam were to be accepted common opinion, European journalists would write away in the Islamic vein. And if spiritual science had grown into a habit of human souls, then the same journalists who today grumble at spiritual science would write very finely in the sense of spiritual science. Today, however, the very people whose task it should be are disinclined to go into such things.

As much as human beings stand here on earth, they are really connected with the whole cosmos. And I have said before that what is true today on earth has not always been true. To mention only the most important points, we shall speak principally now of the period since the great Atlantean flood (geology calls it the Ice Age). We know that changes took place in humanity at that time, but there had been a humanity before, albeit in a different form. (You can read how humans lived then in *Occult Science*.) The Atlantean evolution preceded the present evolution. For instance, where the Atlantic Ocean is now, used to be land. A great part of Europe was under the sea—conditions on earth were quite different during the age of this Atlantean humanity. The ancient Atlantean civilization disappeared; The post-Atlantean has taken its place. But the Atlantean had followed the so-called Lemurian civilization, which in turn had several epochs. Thus we can say that we are in the fifth post-Atlantean civilization, following the first, second, third, and fourth epochs. Before this, there was the Atlantean civilization with its seven epochs (see diagram below), before this again, the Lemurian civilization with its seven epochs. Let us turn our attention to the seven epochs of the Lemurian civilization, which lies approximately 25,900 years before our era. The seventh epoch of the Lemurian civilization came to an end about 25,000 to 26,000 years ago.

Remarkable as it may sound, there is a certain resemblance between this seventh Lemurian epoch and our own. As we know, similarities are always to be found, of the most diverse kinds. We have found a close similarity between our epoch and the Egypto-Chaldean epoch. We are now speaking of a much more far-flung similarity: there is in any case an external cosmic link. You know that our epoch, which begins about the fifteenth century of the Christian era, is connected with the cosmos through the fact that since that time the sun has its vernal point in Pisces, in the constellation of the Fish. Previously, for 2,160 years, the sun had been in the constellation of Aries, the Ram, at the vernal equinox. In this seventh Lemurian epoch there were similar conditions. Twelve epochs ago, the sun was in the same position, so that toward the end of the Lemurian epoch conditions were similar to ours.

However, this similarity covers important differences. What we acquire today in the way of inner forces of spirit and intellectual experience, as we have described them in these studies, was also experienced by the Lemurian human being, though in a different manner. The Lemurian human was constitutionally very different from the human of today. Whatever could enter from the universe really penetrated right in. The Lemurian received practically the same content of wisdom as the human being of today receives through the head, but it streamed into the Lemurian directly from the universe; this was the only difference. The Lemurian's head was still open, the head still susceptible to the conditions of the cosmos. Powers of clairvoyance existed in those ancient times. Human beings did not explain things logically to themselves; they did not learn them, but they beheld them, since things entered the head straight from the cosmos, whereas now they can no longer do so. For now, what comes in can enter the head directly only in early childhood. As I have said, the head no longer stands in such intimate connection with the cosmos, whereas at that time the human head

stood in much more inward relation to the universe; at
that time, the human being still received world wisdom.
This does not mean that it lacked the logic which is nevertheless lacking in what humans gain for themselves nowadays. That original wisdom was actually inspired; it came to
the human from without, arising from divine worlds.
Present-day humans are unwilling to consider this; for
modern people believe (forgive me again if I express
myself somewhat drastically) that ever since they have been
on earth their skull has been as hard as it is today. This is
not true. The head has closed only relatively recently. In
ancient times, it was responsive to the streams of cosmic
influences. By now, all that is left is an atavistic remainder.
Everyone who has observed a really young child's head has
noted there is still one soft place. This is the last relic of
that openness to the cosmos, the place where in ancient
times cosmic forces worked in a certain way into the head,
and gave cosmic wisdom. At that time, human beings did
not need the correspondence with the heart, for they had
a small heart in the head that has become shrivelled and
rudimentary by now. Thus do human beings change. But
conditions alter over the earth, and humans must understand this and change too, adapt themselves to changed
conditions. If our head had not ossified, we would have
been perpetually tied to the apron-strings of the cosmos.
As it is, we have been shut off from the cosmos and can
develop an independent ego. It is important to bear this in
mind. We can develop an independent ego by reason of
having acquired physically this hard skull. We may ask
when humanity actually lost the last remnant of the memories, the living memories of ancient archetypal wisdom.
This remnant really faded away only in the epoch preced-
ing ours, the fourth post-Atlantean epoch, that of the
Greco-Roman civilization. By then humans had long since
possessed closed skulls, but the Mysteries still preserved

the original wisdom preserved from quite ancient times, from the epoch that preceded the Lemurian Pisces age, the Lemurian Aries age.

Whatever ego Lemurian humans could have was also revealed from the cosmos; the individual's inmost soul force was manifested from the cosmos. This ended in the fourth post-Atlantean epoch, the Greco-Latin time. The heavens closed their last door to human beings. Instead, they sent down their great Messenger precisely at that time, so that humans could find on earth what until then was received from heaven: the Christ. The Mystery of Golgotha is a cosmic fact, insofar as without it there would have ceased for humanity what had been revealed from the heavens, cosmically revealed since the Lemurian time. Therefore the impulse which can reveal cosmic wisdom on the earth appeared. Now, the human being must gradually develop what has been revealed on earth in the Christ-Impulse, develop it precisely by that process of rejuvenation of which we have been speaking.

A result of this human development is that we bear something within us today that is, one can say, quite wonderful. I have already mentioned in yesterday's lecture that the knowledge of our time is the most spiritual possible; however human beings do not notice it because they do not let it mature. What can be known today about nature is far more spiritual than was ever formerly known. What humans knew before brought down certain realities from the cosmos. In the stars, as I mentioned yesterday, the Scholastics of the Middle Ages still saw angelic Intelligences. Modern mathematics no longer sees angelic Intelligences of course, but something that can be calculated mathematically or mechanically. But it is as if what used to be seen has been sifted, thoroughly passed through the finest sieve, down to the last trace of spirituality. Actually Novalis's lovable genius was needed to see this rightly. In his

Aphorisms, you find the beautiful expression, which I have often quoted: "Mathematics is in truth a great poem." But to see how mathematics, by which one also calculates the worlds of the stars and their courses, can be a great poem, one must be a poet oneself, not like the modern natural scientists, but a poet like Novalis. Then one stands in awe before the poetry of mathematics. For mathematics is phantasy. Mathematics is nothing observable through the senses, it is phantasy. It is, however, the final product of a phantasy that still is connected with the immediate external reality. Mathematics, in fact, is maya passed through the finest of sieves. And if one learns to know it, not merely the way today's schoolmasters see it, but to know it in its substance, by what it can reveal, then indeed one learns to know something that has as little reality as the image we see in the mirror placed in front of us, but which nevertheless, in certain circumstances, can tell us a great deal. But to be sure, only a fool would consider the image in the mirror final reality. And if one wants to hold a conversation with the reflection because one confuses it with reality, then one is not looking for reality in the right place. Equally as little can reality be found in the astronomers' mathematical calculations. Just as the mirror-image cannot exist without the reality, so the whole spiritual existence, as calculated purely mathematically, is not really there; it is completely sifted, distilled, and must force its way back to reality.

Precisely because our age has become so abstract, because it has been shaped so purely by the head, it has immense spiritual content. And nothing is quite as purely spiritual as the science of the present, only people do not know, or value, that fact. At any rate, it is almost ridiculous to be materialistic with modern science! It is actually rather strange to go through life taking modern science materialistically, yet almost all scholars do take it thus. Given the kind of concepts that modern science can develop, it is comical to assert that there is only material existence; for if there really were only matter, it would not be possible to assert that there was material existence. The very fact of making the statement "matter exists," this action of the soul, is the finest spirituality possible. It is proof in itself that there is more than material existence. One can assert all kinds of things, but if one really assumes that existence is purely material, one can never assert that there is a material existence. The very assertion is in itself proof that one is talking nonsense. For if, as the materialist claims, there were truly only material existence, nothing could ever arise out of that material existence which could result in any way in someone saying "matter exists" for this very saying is a spiritual process.

As you can see, no better logical proof has ever been provided for the world being of the spirit than is being provided by the science of our time, which does not believe in the spirit—which means it does not believe in itself—and by our whole age, which does not believe in itself. Only because humanity has spiritualized itself increasingly from epoch to epoch and has arrived at the sharply refined concepts that we have today, only because of this has humanity reached the point of seeing the finely "sifted" concepts and—of its own volition—connecting them with the forces of the heart. This is shown very clearly by concrete life; it is shown also by the catastrophic events of our time.

If one really studies history, one sees an enormous difference between what we now call the world war—which is really no war at all, but something else—and earlier wars. People do not yet pay any attention to these things, but the distinction is already plain to see in everything that is going on. One could bring up many proofs that this is the case. But many people speak very unclearly while using a quite particular acuity, like the man from whose article I read an extract. And this contemporary mental acuity is what gets people to say time and time again things like, "The war must be prolonged as long as possible so that the best possible peace can be established." No one would have said things like that in earlier wars. And in many other respects no one would have spoken the way people speak today. As I said earlier, people do not notice it yet, but it is true nevertheless. If you take all earlier wars, you will find that fundamentally, in some way or another, people were able to say why they were waging war. I will give two examples only, although hundreds are available. People before wanted something to be definite, clearly outlined, described. Can people today do this? And if they can, do they do it? Many of those heavily involved in the war do not do it. No one knows what really lies behind things. And if people say that they want this or that, they formulate it in such a way that the other side has no real idea what they want.

That was certainly not the case in earlier wars. You could go through the whole of world history and not find anything like it. You can take such grievous events in earlier times as, say, the invasions of Europe by the Tartars, the Mongols, and you will always find that there were quite definite goals, which could be sharply defined, which could be understood, and from which one could understand what was really happening. Where today is there a clear definition of what is actually going on?

This is one thing. But now, something else—What was generally the result of earlier wars? Look wherever you will and you will find that they resulted in some territorial change, which people then accepted. How do people face these things today? They all explain that there must be no territorial change. So one must ask oneself, "What was the whole thing for?" Compared with the past, this is really where things stand: People cannot fight for the things they always fought for, for that is simply not done. The moment something is supposed to happen someone instantly declares "That simply cannot be done." Thus according to the prevailing impulses no real peace is possible; for if one were to leave everything as it was before, there was no need to begin the war in the first place. But since one has begun, and nevertheless wants to leave everything as it was before, one naturally can't leave off, for otherwise there would have been no need to begin!

These things are abstract and paradoxical, but they correspond to profound realities; they correspond to conditions that ought to be kept in mind at the present time. One must in fact say that what is discussed here as the lack of correspondence between head-human and heart-human is a world-historical fact. On the other hand, one can also say that humanity is in a quite particular stage of development: human beings cannot control their thoughts in a human way. That is the most significant characteristic of our time; human beings cannot humanly control their thoughts. All has changed, and people are not yet willing to notice that it has.

Thus we are concerned not merely with something that has to do with world conceptions, but something that very deeply affects the most widespread event of our time, the most crushing event for humanity. People no longer find out from their own souls the connection with their own thoughts. And this shows us how not only the individual but humanity as a whole has forgotten how to mobilize the rejuvenating forces. Humanity will not easily extricate itself from this condition. It can do so only if we believe in the rejuvenating forces, and if we can get rid of those things that cannot be rejuvenated. Whether we look at individuals or at our surroundings, we find everywhere the same thing. We find a sifted head wisdom, head experience, without the will to let things ripen through the heart's experience. This, however, is so deeply linked with the needs of the common evolution of humanity that we must turn our closest attention to it for the present and immediate future.

We have indeed often spoken of it previously from the most varied points of view. Precisely this state of things shows how necessary it is for spiritual science to enter the world today—even as something abstract. But spiritual science is fruitful; it can reform the world because it can send its impulse into actual concrete conditions of life. Humanity faces a sad future if people no longer have faith in becoming older, if they want to stop short at what can be experienced by the short-lived head. I have said already that the utmost that can be attained by the short-lived head is abstract socialism, unrelated to concrete conditions. Yet this is really the only thing people believe in. Philosophers are constantly telling us nothing exists but matter—due to the philosophers' own finely tuned spirituality. Of course, they should better give up that judgment at once, for it is pure nonsense. The mainspring of the present so-called war is to be found in general world conditions from which there is no way out—just as there is no way out from the sentence "There is only matter." For the present time is in fact of the spirit! And the spiritual element in this time needs condensing, strengthening, so that it can affect reality; otherwise, it will remain a mirror image. The way humanity works today is as if we didn't want to work in a workshop with real men and women, instead believing it possible to work in a workshop with mirror images of men and women.

That is true of the most extreme form of cerebral socialism, which is what makes it so illuminating for great masses of people, since it is all logical intellectual experience, purely logical head experience. But if this logical head experience cannot meet the spiritual element in the other person, what then can it meet? I have repeatedly spoken of that, and again today. It unites with the blind desires and instincts. Then an impure mixture results between the head experience, which is really quite spiritual, and the blind instincts and desires. That union is what some are now trying to achieve in the East! The purely cerebral socialist theory has nothing to do with the actual concrete conditions of the East; what men like Lenin and Trotsky have devised has nothing to do with what is developing out of concrete necessity in the East. If through some peculiar chain of circumstances, Lenin and Trotsky had landed in Australia instead of Russia, they would have thought they could introduce the same conditions that they wish to introduce in Russia. The conditions fit Australia, or South America, just as much, or as little as they do Russia; they would fit just as well on the moon, since they fit no real concrete conditions. Why? Because they come from the head, and the head is not of the earth. Perhaps they really *would* fit better on the moon since they are purely of the head. That they are intelligible comes from the fact that they are closely related to the head. But here on earth such things must be established as are related to the earth; we must find a spirituality which is connected with the earth's future, in the way we described yesterday.

This leads us into deep and significant matters. And when we consider them, we will see how little inclined people today really are to go into these matters. Yet they are as necessary as daily bread. Otherwise, if we cannot find the path to rejuvenation, the evolution of humanity will lead either to the pit, or to a blind alley.

24 December 1920

IN THE FESTIVAL of Christmas something is given to Christendom that directs the thoughts of all circles of Christian people straight to the very deepest questions presented by the evolution of humankind upon earth. Regard the evolution of history from whatever point of view you will, take into consideration historical events in order to understand human evolution, to penetrate the meaning of human evolution on earth—in all history you will find no thought as widely understandable or having as much power to lift the soul to this mystery of human evolution as the thought of the Mystery of Golgotha, as the thought that is contained in the festival of Christmas.

When we look back upon the beginning of human evolution on earth, and follow it through the thousands of years that preceded the Mystery of Golgotha, we find that, although the achievements of the peoples in all the various nations were so great, nevertheless, in reality all these achievements constituted only a kind of preparation—they were a preparatory step toward what took place for the sake of humankind at the Mystery of Golgotha. Furthermore, we find we can only understand what has happened since the Mystery of Golgotha when we remember that the Christ who went through the Mystery of Golgotha has played an active role in the evolution of humanity ever since. Many things in human evolution may at first appear incomprehensible. However, if we investigate them without narrow-minded superstition, for example the kind of superstition that believes that unknown gods should come to the aid of human beings without their active involvement, and that such aid should come just where human beings consider it necessary—if we leave aside such views, we find that even the most painful events in the course of world history can show us the significance and meaning that the evolution of the earth has acquired through the fact that Christ went through the Mystery of Golgotha. It is appropriate for us to study this Mystery of Golgotha—and the mystery of Christmas belongs to it—from a point of view which can reveal, as it were, the meaning of all of earthly humanity. We know how intimate the connection is between what takes place in the moral-spiritual sphere of human evolution and what takes place in nature. And with a certain understanding of this link between nature and the world's moral order we can approach also another relationship with which we have been concerned for many years—namely, the relationship of Christ Jesus to that being whose outer reflection appears in the sun. The followers and representatives of the Christian impulse were not always so hostile toward the recognition of this connection between the mystery of the sun and the mystery of Christ as the decadent present-day representatives of Christianity so often are. Dionysius the Areopagite, whom we have often mentioned, calls the sun God's monument, and in Augustine we continually find such allusions. Even in Scholasticism we find such references to the fact that the outwardly visible stars and their movements are images of the divine-spiritual existence of the world.

However, we must understand the mystery of Christmas in a far wider context, if we wish to understand what should concern us most of all in view of the important tasks of the present age. I would like to remind you of something which I have repeatedly brought forward in various ways in the course of many years. I have told you: We look back into the first post-Atlantean age, which was filled with the deeds and experiences of the ancient Indian people; we look back into the ancient Persian epoch of post-Atlantean humanity, into the Egypto-Chaldean, and into the Greco-Latin. We come then to the fifth epoch of the post-Atlantean humanity, our own. Our epoch will be followed by the sixth and by the seventh. And I have drawn your attention to the fact that the Greco-Latin, the fourth epoch of post-Atlantean humanity, stands, as it were, in the middle, and that there are certain connections (you can read of this in my little book *The Spiritual Guidance of the Individual and Humanity*) between the third and the fifth epochs, that is, between the Egyptio-Chaldean epoch and our own. Furthermore there is also a certain connection between the ancient Persian epoch and the sixth, and between the ancient Indian and the seventh epoch of post-Atlantean humanity. Specific things repeat themselves in a certain way in each of these epochs of life.

I once pointed out that the great Kepler, the successor of Copernicus, had a feeling that his solar and planetary system was repeating, of course in a way appropriate to the fifth post-Atlantean age, what had lived as the world picture behind the Egyptian priest mysteries. Kepler himself expressed this in a certain sense very radically when he said that he had borrowed the vessels of the ancient Egyptian teachers of wisdom in order to carry them over into the new age.

Today, however, we will consider something which stood, in a sense, at the center of the view found in the cultic rituals performed by the priests in the Egyptian mystery religion; we will consider the mysteries of Isis. In order to call up before our minds the spiritual connection between the mystery of Isis and that which also lives in Christianity, we need only look with the eyes of the soul upon Raphael's famous picture of the Sistine Madonna. The Virgin is holding the child Jesus, and behind her are the clouds, representing a multitude of children. We can imagine the Virgin receiving the child Jesus descending through the clouds, through a condensation, as it were, of the thin cloud substance. Created out of an entirely Christian spirit, this picture is, after all, nothing more than a kind of repetition of what the Egyptian mysteries of Isis revered when they portrayed Isis holding the child Horus. The motif of that earlier picture is in complete harmony with that of Raphael's picture. Of course, this fact must not tempt us to a superficial interpretation, common among many people since the eighteenth century and throughout the nineteenth century right up to our own days—namely, to see the story of Christ Jesus and all that belongs to it as a mere metamorphosis, a transformation, of ancient pagan mysteries. From my book *Christianity as Mystical Fact* you already know how these things are to be understood. However, in the sense explained in that book we are permitted to point out a spiritual congruence between what appears in Christianity and the old pagan mysteries.

The main content of the mystery of Isis is the death of Osiris and Isis's search for the dead Osiris. We know that Osiris, the representative of the being of the sun, the representative of the spiritual sun, is killed by Typhon, who, expressed in Egyptian terms, is none other than Ahriman. Ahriman kills Osiris, throws him into the Nile, and the Nile carries the body away. Isis, the spouse of Osiris, sets out on her search and finds him over in Asia. She brings him back to Egypt, where Ahriman, the enemy, cuts the body into fourteen parts. Isis buries these fourteen parts in various locations, so that they belong to the earth for ever after.

We can see from this story how Egyptian wisdom conceived of the connection between the powers of heaven
and the powers of earth in a deeply meaningful way. On
the one hand, Osiris is the representative of the powers of
the sun. After having passed through death he is, in various places and simultaneously, the force that ripens everything that grows out of the earth. The ancient Egyptian
sage imagines in a spirit-filled way how the powers which
shine down from the sun, enter the earth and then
become part of the earth, and how, as powers of the sun
buried in the earth, they then hand over to the human
being what matures out of the earth. The Egyptian myth is
founded upon the story of Osiris—how he was killed, how
his spouse Isis had to set out on her search for him, how
she first brought him back to Egypt and how he then
became active in another form, namely, from out of the
earth.

One of the Egyptian pyramids depicts the whole event
in a particularly meaningful way. The Egyptians not only
recorded what they knew as the solution to the great
secrets of the universe in their own particular writing, they
also expressed it in their architectural constructions. They
built one of these pyramids with such mathematical preci-
sion that the shadow of the sun disappeared into the base
of the pyramid at the spring equinox and only reappeared
at the autumn equinox. The Egyptians wanted to express
in this pyramid that the forces which shine down from the
sun are buried from spring to fall in the earth where they
develop the forces of the earth, so that the earth may produce the fruit which humankind needs.

This, then, is the idea we find present in the minds and
hearts of the ancient Egyptians. On the one hand, they
look up to the sun, they look up to the lofty being of the
sun and they worship him. At the same time, however, they
relate how this being of the sun was lost in Osiris, and was

sought by Isis, and how he was found again so that he is then able to continue working in a changed way.

Many things which appeared in the Egyptian wisdom must be repeated in a different form during our fifth post-Atlantean age. Humankind must increasingly come to understand from a spiritual-scientific point of view the mysteries of the Egyptian priests in a form appropriate to our own age, in a Christian sense. For the Egyptians, Osiris was a kind of representative of the Christ who had not yet arrived on earth. In their own way they looked upon Osiris as the being of the sun, but they imagined this sun being had been lost in a sense, and must be found again. We cannot imagine that our being of the sun, the Christ, who has passed through the Mystery of Golgotha could be lost to humankind, for he came down from spiritual heights, united himself with the man Jesus of Nazareth, and from then onwards remains with the earth. He is present, he exists, as the Christmas carol proclaims each year anew: "Unto us a Saviour is born." It thereby expresses the eternal, not the transitory nature of this event. Jesus was not only born once at Bethlehem, but is born continuously; in other words, he remains with the life of the earth. What Christ is, and what he means for us, cannot be lost.

But the Isis legend must show itself as being fulfilled in another way in our time. We cannot lose the Christ and what he, in a higher form than Osiris, gives us; but we can lose, and we have lost, what is portrayed for our Christian understanding standing at the side of Osiris—Isis—the mother of the saviour, the divine wisdom, Sophia. If the Isis legend is to be renewed, then it must not simply follow the old form—Osiris, killed by Typhon-Ahriman and carried away by the waters of the Nile, must be found again by Isis in order that his body, cut into pieces by Typhon-Ahriman, may be sunk into the earth. No, in a sense, we must find the Isis legend again, the content of the mystery of Isis, but we must create it out of imagination, suited to our own times. An understanding must arise again of the eternal cosmic truths, and it will when we learn to think and compose imaginatively, as the Egyptians did. But we must find the right Isis legend.

The Egyptian was permeated by luciferic powers, as were all human beings who lived before the Mystery of Golgotha. If luciferic powers are within the human being and stir the inner life, moving and weaving through it, the result will then be that ahrimanic powers will appear as an active force outside the human being. Thus the Egyptians, who were themselves permeated by Lucifer, rightly see a picture of the world in which Ahriman-Typhon is active.

Now, we must realize that modern humanity is permeated by Ahriman. Ahriman moves and surges within human beings, just as Lucifer moved and surged within the Egyptian world. However, when Ahriman works through Lucifer, then human beings see their picture of the world in a luciferic form. How does the human being see this picture of the world? This luciferic picture of the world has been created, it is here. It has become increasingly popular for modern times and has taken hold of all circles of people who want to consider themselves progressive and enlightened.

If the mystery of Christmas is to be understood, we must bear in mind that Lucifer is the power wanting to retain the world-picture of an earlier stage. Lucifer is the power trying to bring into the modern world-conception that which existed in earlier stages of human development. He wants to give permanence to what existed in earlier periods. All that was moral in earlier stages also exists of course today. (The significance of morality always lies in the present, where, like seeds for the future, it provides the basis for the creation of worlds yet to come.) But Lucifer strives to separate morality as such, all moral forces, from our world picture. He allows the laws of natural necessity alone to appear in our picture of the external world. Thus the impoverished human being of modern times is presented with a wisdom of the world in which the stars move according to purely mechanical necessity, in which the stars are devoid of morality, so that the moral meaning of the world's order cannot be found in their movements. This, my dear friends, is a purely luciferic world picture.

Just as the Egyptians looked out into the world and saw Ahriman-Typhon as the one who takes Osiris away from them, so too, we must look at our luciferic world picture, at the mathematical-mechanical world picture of modern-day astronomy and other branches of natural science, and realize that the luciferic element holds sway in this world picture, just as the typhonic-ahrimanic element held sway in the Egyptian world picture. Just as the ancient Egyptians saw their outer world picture in an ahrimanic-typhonic light, so modern human beings, because they are ahrimanic, see it with luciferic characteristics. Lucifer is present, he is working there. Just as the Egyptians imagined Ahriman-Typhon working in wind and weather, in the storms of winter, so modern human beings, if they wish to truly understand the world, must imagine that Lucifer appears to them in the sunshine and in the light of the stars, in the movements of the planets and of the moon. The world picture of Copernicus, Galileo, and Kepler is a luciferic construction. Precisely because it arose from and corresponds to our ahrimanic forces of knowledge, its content—please distinguish here between method and content—is a luciferic one.

When the Mystery of Golgotha took place, the divine Sophia, the wisdom that enables us to see into the world with understanding, worked in a twofold way. Divine wisdom, heavenly wisdom, worked in the revelation to the poor shepherds in the fields, and in the revelation to the wise men from the East. This wisdom was still present in its later form among the Gnostics, from whom the early Christian fathers and teachers of the Church took this wisdom and used it to understand the Mystery of Golgotha. This wisdom could not be continued into our times. It was overwhelmed and killed by Lucifer, just as Osiris was killed by Ahriman-Typhon. We have not lost Osiris, that is, the Christ, we have lost that being who for us takes the place of Isis. Lucifer has killed her. But the Isis being killed by Lucifer was not sunk into the earth, as Typhon sunk Osiris into the Nile. Lucifer carried the Isis being, the divine wisdom whom he had killed, out into the world's spaces; he sunk her into the ocean of space. When we look out into this ocean and only see the stars moving according to mathematical lines, then we see the grave of what spiritually permeated this world, for the divine Sophia, the successor of Isis, is dead.

We must create this legend, for it presents the truth of our times. We must speak of the dead and lost Isis, the divine Sophia, in the same way that ancient Egyptians spoke of the dead and lost Osiris. With the power we do not understand but which nevertheless is in us, with the power of Christ, the power of the new Osiris, we must set out in search of the dead body of the modern Isis, the dead body of the divine Sophia. We must approach luciferic natural science and seek there the coffin of Isis; in other words, in what natural science gives us we must find something which stimulates us inwardly toward Imagination, Inspiration, and Intuition. In this way we acquire the help of Christ within—Christ, who remains hidden for us in darkness if we do not illuminate him with divine wisdom. Armed with this power of Christ, with the new Osiris, we must set out in search of Isis, the new Isis. Lucifer will not cut Isis in pieces, as Ahriman-Typhon did with Osiris; on the contrary, this Isis is spread out in her true form in the beauty of the whole universe. This Isis shines out of the cosmos in an aura of many luminous colors. We must learn to understand Isis when we look out into the cosmos, to see this cosmos in its aura of luminous colors.

But just as Ahriman-Typhon once cut Osiris into pieces, so Lucifer comes to blur and wash out the colors in all their clear distinctness; he blends and merges into one single whole the parts which are so beautifully distributed over the heavens, the limbs of the new Isis which go to make the great firmament of the heavens. Just as Typhon cut Osiris into pieces, so Lucifer blends the manifold colors that stream down to us from the aura of the universe into a uniform white light that radiates through the universe. This is the light that Goethe fought against in his theory of colors, opposing the statement that white light contains all the colors, which in truth extend over the mysterious, manifold and secret deeds of the whole universe.

But we must persevere in our search until we again find Isis. And when we have found her, we must find a way to place into the universe what we are then able to discover and to know. What we acquire through the newly found Isis, we must place before our souls in a living way, so that the whole universe, the cosmos, becomes spiritual for us again. We must understand Saturn, Sun, Moon, Earth, Jupiter, Venus, and Vulcan from within. What Lucifer has made of Isis, we must transfer into the heavenly spaces just as Isis buried in the earth parts of the body of Osiris, cut into pieces by Typhon-Ahriman. We must realize that through the power of Christ we can find an inner astronomy that will show us the universe proceeding from and working out of the power of the spirit. Then the rediscovered power of Isis, which is now the power of the divine Sophia, will allow Christ, who has united with the earth since the Mystery of Golgotha, to become active in the new insight into the universe, to become active within us because of our new knowledge. We do not lack Christ; but the knowledge of Christ, the Sophia of Christ, the Isis of Christ is lacking.

This is what we should engrave in our souls as a content of the mystery of Christmas. We must realize that since the nineteenth century even theology has come to look upon Christ merely as the man from Nazareth. That means that theology is completely permeated by Lucifer. It no longer sees into the spiritual background of existence. External natural science is luciferic; theology is luciferic. Of course if we are speaking of the inner aspect of the human being as you can see from my previous words we could just as well say that in this theology the human being is ahrimanic. Then in the same way we must say of the Egyptians that they were luciferic, just as we say of them that their perception of the external world was ahrimanic. Modern human beings must understand the mystery of Christmas in a new way. They must realize that they must first of all seek Isis, in order that Christ may appear to them. The cause of our misfortunes and the problems of modern civilization is not that we have lost Christ, who stands before us in a far greater glory than Osiris did in the eyes of the Egyptians. It is not that we have lost him and need to set out in search of him, armed with the force of Isis. No, what we have lost is the knowledge of Christ Jesus, insight into his being. This is what we must find again with the power of the Jesus Christ who is in us.

This is how we must look upon the content of the Christmas festival. For many modern people Christmas is nothing more than a festival for giving and receiving presents, something which they celebrate every year through habit. Like so many other things in modern life the Christmas festival has become an empty phrase. And it is just because so many things have become nothing more than a phrase that modern life is so full of calamities and chaos.

This is in truth the deeper reason for the chaos in our modern life.

If in this our community, we could acquire the right feelings for everything which has become mere phrases in the present age, and if these feelings could enable us to find the impulses needed for the renewals that are so necessary, then this community, which calls itself the anthroposophical community, would be worthy of its existence. This community should understand the terrible significance for our age that such things as the Christmas festival are carried forward as a mere phrase. We should be able to understand that in the future this must not be allowed, and that these things must be given a new content. Old habits must be left behind and new insights must take their place. If we cannot find the inner courage needed to do this, then we share in the lie which keeps up the yearly Christmas festival merely as a phrase, celebrating it without our souls feeling and sensing the true significance of the event. Are we really lifted up to the highest concerns of humanity when we give and receive presents every year out of habit at this festival of Christ? Do we lift ourselves up to the highest concerns of humanity when we listen to the words—which have also become a phrase—spoken by the representatives of the various religious communities! We should forbid ourselves to continue in this inner hollowness of our Christmas celebrations. We should make the inner decision to give such a festival a content which allows the highest, worthiest feelings to pass through our souls. Such a festival celebration would raise humankind to the comprehension of the meaning of its existence.

Ask yourselves whether the feelings in your hearts and souls when you stand before the Christmas tree and open the presents which are given out of habit, and the Christmas cards containing the usual phrases—ask yourselves whether feelings are living in you that can raise human-kind to an understanding of the meaning of its evolution on earth! All the problems and misfortune of our time are due to this—we cannot find the courage to lift ourselves above the empty phrases of our age. But it must happen, a new content must come—a content which can give us entirely new feelings that stir us powerfully, just as those people were stirred who were true Christians in the first Christian centuries, and who felt the Mystery of Golgotha and the appearance of Christ as the highest which human-kind could experience upon the earth. Our souls must again acquire something of this spirit.

Oh, the soul will attain to altogether new feelings if it feels committed to experience the new Isis legend within modern humanity. Lucifer kills Isis and then places her body into the infinity of space, which has become the grave of Isis, a mathematical abstraction. Then comes the search for Isis, and her discovery, made possible through the inner force of spiritual knowledge. In place of the heavens that have become dead, this knowledge places what stars and planets reveal through an inner life, so that they then appear as monuments to the spiritual powers that weave with power through space. We are able to look at the man-ger today in the right way only if we experience in a unique way what is weaving with spiritual power through space, and then look at that being who came into the world through the child. We know that we bear this being within us, but we must also understand him. Just as the Egyptians looked from Osiris to Isis, so we must learn to look again to the new Isis, the holy Sophia. Christ will appear again in his spiritual form during the course of the twentieth cen-tury, not through the arrival of external events alone, but because human beings find the power represented by the holy Sophia. The modern age has had the tendency to lose this power of Isis, this power of Mary. It has been killed by all that arose with the modern consciousness of human-kind. And the confessions have in part exterminated just this view of Mary.

This is the mystery of modern humanity: Fundamentally speaking, Mary-Isis has been killed, and she must be sought, just as Osiris was sought by Isis in Asia. But she must be sought in the infinite spaces of the universe with the power that Christ can awaken in us, if we devote ourselves to him in the right way.

Let us picture this rightly, let us immerse ourselves in this new Isis legend which must be experienced, and let us fill our souls with it. Then we will experience in a true sense what humankind in many of its representatives believes, that this new legend fills the holy eve of Christmas, in order to bring us into Christmas day, the day of Christ. This anthroposophical community could become a community of human beings united in love because they feel the need, common to them all, to search. Let us become conscious of this most intimate task! Let us go in spirit to the manger and bring to the Child our sacrifice and our gift, which lie in the knowledge that something altogether new must fill our souls, in order that we may fulfill the tasks which can lead humankind out of barbarism into a truly new civilization.

To achieve this, of course, it is absolutely necessary that in our circles we are prepared to help one another in love, so that a real community of souls arises in which all forms of envy and the like disappear, and in which we do not look merely each at the other, but together face the great goal we have in common. The mystery brought into the world by the Christmas child also contains this—that we can look at a common goal without discord because the common goal signifies union in harmony. The light of Christmas should actually shine as a light of peace, as a light that brings external peace, only because first of all it brings an inner peace into the hearts of human beings. We should learn to say to ourselves: If we can manage to work together in love on the great tasks, then, and only then, do we understand Christmas. If we cannot manage this, we do not understand Christmas.

Let us remember that when we do sow discord, this discord hinders us in understanding the one who appeared among human beings on the first Christmas on earth. Can we not pour this mystery of Christmas into our souls, as something which unites our hearts in love and harmony? If we do not properly understand what spiritual science is, then we will not be able to do this. Nothing will come of this community if we merely bring into it ideas and impulses we have picked up here and there from all corners of the world, where clichés and routine hold sway. Let us remember that our community is facing a difficult year, that all our forces must be gathered together, and let us celebrate Christmas in this spirit. Oh, I would like to find words that could speak deeply into the heart of each one of you on this evening. Then each one of you would feel that my words contain a greeting which is at the same time an appeal to kindle spiritual science within your hearts, so that it may become a power that can help humanity which is living under such terrible oppression.

Beginning with such points of view, I have gathered the thoughts which I wished to speak to you. Be assured that they are intended as a warm Christmas greeting for each one of you, as something which can lead you into the new year in the very best way. In this spirit, accept my words today as they were intended, as an affectionate Christmas greeting.

Isis-Sophia
Des Gottes Weisheit
Sie hat Luzifer getotet
Und auf der Weltenkrafte Schwingen
In Raumesweiten fortgetragen.
Christus-Wollen
In Menschen wirkend;
Es wird Luzifer entreissen
Und auf des Geisteswissens Booten
In Menschenseelen auferwecken
Isis-Sophia
Des Gottes Weisheit.

Isis-Sophia
Wisdom of God:
Lucifer has slain her,
And on the wings of the powers of the world
Carried her hence into the infinite space
    of the universe.
The willing of Christ
Working in man
Shall wrest from Lucifer
And on the boats of Spirit-knowledge
Awaken in human souls
Isis-Sophia
Wisdom of God.

Translated by James H. Hindes

PUBLISHER'S NOTE

The lectures printed here were given by Rudolf Steiner to audiences familiar with the general background and terminology of his anthroposophical teaching. It should be remembered that in his autobiography, *The Course of My Life*, he emphasizes the distinction between his written works on the one hand, and on the other, reports of lectures that were given as oral communications and were not originally intended for print. For an intelligent appreciation of the lectures it should be borne in mind that certain premises were taken for granted when the words were spoken. "These premises," Rudolf Steiner writes, "include at the very least the anthroposophical knowledge of humanity and of the cosmos in its spiritual essence; also what may be called 'anthroposophical history,' told as an outcome of research into the spiritual world."

RUDOLF STEINER (1861–1925) was the founder of Anthroposophy, a modern spiritual path or science. Out of his spiritual researches, he was able to provide indications for the renewal of many human activities, including education (Waldorf Schools), agriculture (Biodynamics), medicine (Anthroposophical Medicine), special education (the Camphill Movement), economics, philosophy, religion, and the arts. In 1924, he founded the General Anthroposophical Society, which today has branches throughout the world.